Shoestring Glory

SHOESTRING GLORY

A *Prairie History* of *Semi-Pro Ball*

Lewis St. George Stubbs

TURNSTONE PRESS

No TOC

Turnstone Press gratefully acknowledges the assistance of
the Canada Council and the Manitoba Arts Council.

Front cover photograph appears courtesy of the Metz Family
Collection. Back cover photographs appear courtesy of Provincial
Archives of Alberta, Provincial Archives of Manitoba and
Saskatchewan Archives Board.

Design: Manuela Dias

This book was printed and bound in Canada
by Friesens for Turnstone Press.

Canadian Cataloguing in Publication Data
Stubbs, Lewis St. George, 1950—

Shoestring glory.

Includes bibliographical references and index.
ISBN 0-88801-189-X

1. Baseball – Prairie Provinces – History. I. Title.

GV863.15.P7S8 1996   796.357'09712   C96-920013-7

Acknowledgements

With its myriad of facts and figures baseball is the trivia buff's dream. My task was made far easier by the tireless efforts of the Society for American Baseball Research and its essential publications like *Total Baseball, The Negro Leagues Book,* and *The Sports Encyclopedia: Baseball.* Miles Wolff and Lloyd Johnson's *The Encyclopedia of Minor League Baseball* provided me with gems that I could not have tracked down in a year of microfilm reading. Baseball fans in Canada owe William Humber a debt of gratitude for his ground-breaking work in tracing the history of the sport in this country.

I wish to thank the staffs of the following institutions: the Provincial Archives of Manitoba, the Legislative Library of Manitoba, the Western Canada Pictorial Index, and the *Winnipeg Free Press.* My employers and co-workers at the Department of Archives and Special Collections at the University of Manitoba provided me with the flexibility to do my research. The staff at InterLibrary Loan at the Elizabeth Dafoe Library were unfailingly pleasant during the time that I was chained to a microfilm reader. I am indebted to the Saskatchewan Archives Board, the Provincial Archives of Alberta, and the Glenbow Archives in Calgary.

Many individuals provided me with generous assistance. I would like to thank Colin MacPhail, Media Communications Coordinator with the Edmonton Trappers; John Traub, Director of Public Relations with the Calgary Cannons; and Karen McInnis, curator at the Manitoba Sports Hall of Fame. Thanks to George Toles for giving the manuscript its title. Not many writers on a shoestring budget get to bring their own professional photographer to games with them, but my buddy Jeff Solylo was only a phone call away and would scale the centre-field wall to get a shot. My final debt of gratitude is to my editor Neil Besner for patiently sifting through my wall of facts and attempting to steer me towards a thematic approach rather than a recitation of every game played on the Prairies in the past century.

Table of Contents

to Lesley

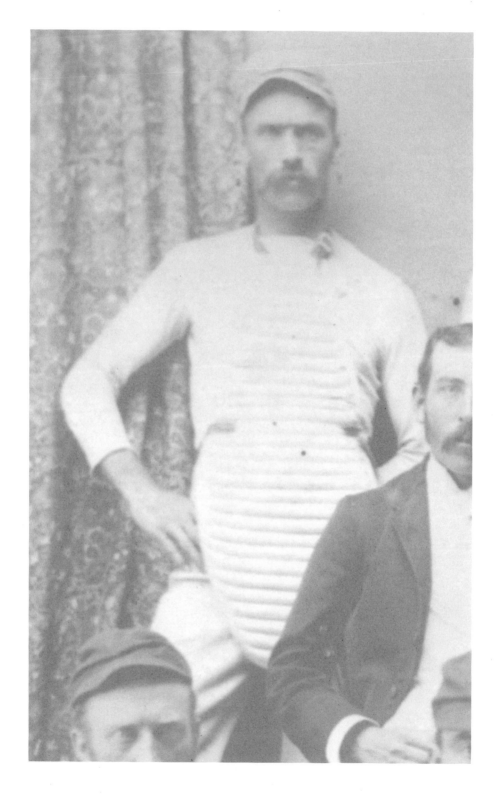

IN THE DAYS
OF MY YOUTH

DESPITE OUR NATIONALISTIC PROTESTS TO THE CONTRARY, HOCKEY IS immediate, never intimate, and seldom nostalgic. Baseball is memories. It's driving your parents to distraction throwing a tennis ball against the front steps and inevitably hitting the front door. Or going to bed with your glove and tossing a hardball up in the air in the dark, working on the night eyes in case you ever played a night game that was hit by a power failure. Errors those nights were twofold: if you dropped the ball on the floor it woke your folks and you were in big trouble, but by far the more common occurrence was taking the ball in the face.

What about those hot summer nights scanning the dial of your transistor radio until you located the faint signal of a game being played in some exotic-sounding place like Kansas City or some other American locale that you were too young to even imagine? Do you remember swapping cards with your buddies on the school steps and having the teacher warn you for the last time to remove your ball cap in class? I recall staring wistfully out the window of our elementary school and praying that my mother's old adage – if there was enough blue in the sky to sew a sailor's suit, there would be no rain that day – was true and Little League wouldn't be cancelled.

Who can forget the unbridled joy of camping under a fly ball, shielding your eyes from the sun and looking it into your glove? We played hours of pepper ball when I was a kid; my buddy Rusen and I had our own variation on the game. The fielder had to handle ten chances in a row to get to bat, and hits nine and ten were line shots guaranteed to maim if you didn't make the play. I had the dual indignity of diving for a hard grounder that I misplayed and being stung by a bee on the same play. Trust me, the error was far more painful. A bad day in the field in the blistering heat could leave a body quite parched. But if you had the prerequisite ten cents, those king-size Cokes out of the drink machine at the local garage tasted mighty fine. The proprietor was a nice enough fellow but he thought I looked like Beaver (as in *Leave It to*), and not Rocky Colovito or some other suitably tough-looking guy.

I can honestly say that I love baseball, for it is the portal that takes me back to the carefree days of childhood. Few feelings could match the tranquillity of sitting in a ballpark on a warm evening at sunset. The eerie glow given off by the stadium lights when they were first turned on slipped the surrounding area into darkness, and seemed to complement the greenness of the manicured outfield grass and the resounding thump that the ball made in the catcher's mitt during the pitcher's warm-up tosses. I relived that experience in the venerable John Ducey Park in Edmonton in the summer of 1994. The evening was a sip of nectar from the fountain of youth as years of cynicism fell away, and for that brief moment, I was back in the late fifties again.

My introduction to baseball was not in the time-honoured custom of playing catch with my father in the backyard. While my dad was merely ambivalent to the game, my mother detested baseball. In her younger days she had witnessed a particularly vulgar contest at Portage la Prairie and held baseball in the high disregard that most parents reserved for pool halls. "Do you want to be a bum and chase a ball all your life?" was her frequent lament. Fortunately, our neighbourhood was teeming with older kids only too willing to have me chase their hits.

Television came late to the Stubbs household. My sister and I had been watching Roy Rogers at the neighbours' for over a year before our mahogany Fleetwood set complete with a radio, gramophone and sliding doors arrived. I have dim recollections of the Milwaukee Braves vs. New York Yankees World Series in 1957 and 1958. My pal Taxy was a bona fide Dodger fan so he was in his glory in '59 when Los Angeles took the Chicago White Sox. Dad would often watch games with me but his hard-and-fast rule was that we always had to cheer for the underdog. This meant rooting against the Yankee juggernaut in summer and the invincible Montreal Canadiens in the winter. Hell, we couldn't even cheer for the hometown Bombers when they were winning all those Grey Cups in the late fifties and early sixties. Many is the night that I was banished to my room over some display of poor sportsmanship.

Things took a turn for the better in 1960. Although I cheered for the St. Louis Cardinals, the major-league affiliate of the Winnipeg Goldeyes, the Pittsburgh Pirates' Roberto Clemente and the Chicago Cubs' Ernie Banks were my two favourite players. Kids nowadays are inundated with trivia about any sports star that they find appealing, but in those days you collected cards or watched the all-star game to get a glimpse of your heroes. Oh sure, there was NBC's "Game of the Week," but ol' Dizzy Dean and Pee Wee Reese spent an inordinate amount of time following those damn Yankees. In 1960, as the players attempted to add revenue to the pension fund, two all-star games were held. The National League won both contests and I got to see Ernie Banks hit a homer; that fall Clemente's Pirates made it to the World Series. Despite being drubbed by scores of 16-3, 10-0, and 12-0 in the contests that they lost, Pittsburgh had home-field advantage for the pivotal seventh and deciding game. While I may have been as big a truant as the next guy during high school, skipping out was not part of my reality in grade four. As there were no night games for the World Series back then, the best a kid could hope for was maybe five innings over the lunch hour. I had to see that game. I bolted back my lunch in record time and dashed to the TV in our living room. The Pirates were up 4-zip after four innings and my mom was doing laundry in the basement. I cut the volume on the game and planned to wring out as many innings as my luck would allow. The Yanks went up 5-4 in the top of the sixth. I could just hear those front-running clowns that I knew back at school rubbing it in. Then things got worse when the Yanks plated two more in the top of the eighth. The situation vastly improving for the Pirates in the bottom half, my mother suddenly appeared in the living room and my situation took a turn for the worse. I tried a stalling tactic and told her it was Yom Kippur. Retreating to the kitchen for the broom, she informed me that we were not Jewish. I hit the door on a dead run. I can't recall if it was a humane teacher or one of the boys with a transistor who broke the news of the Mazeroski Miracle.

I faced a similar dilemma in 1962. Rusen's San Francisco Giants were playing the Yanks in the seventh and deciding game of the World Series. The late start in the Bay area meant early innings at best over the piddly lunch break offered to us overworked grade sixers. When we broke for recess I knew the Yanks were up 1-0. Now I was never considered fast as a kid, but I did that block and a half to our place full blast. What a break: the gods of baseball were smiling upon me! My mother was in the backyard and the Giants were batting in the bottom of the ninth. Matty Alou stood perched on third carrying the tying run, with Willie Mays ninety feet away on second with the series winner. Only a stellar defensive play by Yankee right-fielder Roger Maris had prevented Alou from deadlocking the contest on Mays' double. "Stretch" McCovey faced the 1960 series' goat Ralph Terry with two out. Big Willie already had a homer off of Terry in the second game of the series but all we needed was a lousy single. Could life get any better? I leapt from my chair as Willie lashed a long fly ball to right field; but any victory dance was premature for the ball hooked foul by a couple of feet. A split second later it was over and I was running back to Montrose School cursing. McCovey scalded a liner at Yankee second-sacker Bobby Richardson. Six inches higher and two runs would have scored; six inches lower would have taken Richardson's head off.

Two years later my mother took my sister and me to the New York World's Fair. I recall being vaguely annoyed at having my summer of hanging out with the guys short-circuited. My knowledge of the "Big Apple" consisted of the names of the various sports teams and any local geography purloined from watching *The Bowery Boys* on television. While the World's Fair was neater than I thought it would be, the biggest thrill came when my uncle Bryce took me to see the marvellous Mets play Roberto Clemente's Pittsburgh Pirates. I had my one and only live glimpse at the immense talent of Clemente, who captured the batting title that season.

Puberty might have screwed up some guys' priorities but I was loyal to my game. Rusen and I had plenty of time for inane conversations in those halcyon days before summer jobs. After a particularly vigorous afternoon of shagging flies, he posed this challenge to adolescent fantasy: "So Stubbsy, what would you take – a night with Raquel Welch or a diving grab in the World Series?" Vegas oddsmakers wouldn't have made book on either possibility. In keeping with the self-delusion of the moment I assured him that Raquel was probably a lovely person but hey, we were talking World Series.

I feel like a curmudgeon saying this, but pro baseball was more fun thirty years ago. I loved those drab off-white home-team or grey visitors' flannel jerseys that the players used to wear in the old Northern League. If you caught a foul ball back then you got a free ticket to a game because balls were comparatively expensive. Ballparks like Wrigley Field and Fenway Park had competition for "shrine" status from places like Pittsburgh's Forbes Field, Crosley in Cincinnati and Sportsmen's Park in St. Louis. A ball field was just that, not a tasteless sports complex like the mausoleums inspired by the mindless architecture that cropped up in the early seventies.

Today you have guys playing in teal uniforms, often with matching coloured batting gloves – which are not to be confused with the special sliding gloves they wear when running the base paths. Look at the faces of old-time ballplayers in some of the wonderful pictorial histories available today. In their classic album *Desperado*, the Eagles equate musicians' lives on the road to those of the outlaws of the old West. For me the true desperadoes were the ballplayers that I saw growing up, whose weather-beaten faces could have come off a most-wanted poster. Few minor leaguers could have been cast as matinee idols; they bore a closer resemblance to the guy who played Blackie or Duggan in the weekly *Horse Opera*. Managers looked like Jingles Devine or Dub Taylor, the actors playing the hero's sidekick.

No era can claim a monopoly on talented players, as every generation of ballplayers has had its share of bad actors. Ty Cobb, a bigoted Southerner from Georgia, was never in any danger of being mistaken for Albert Schweitzer on or off the field. Babe Ruth was an oversized man-child who did everything to excess. Sadly we recently witnessed what years of being a "good old boy" can do to a body with the untimely demise of Mickey Mantle. They might not have been the greatest role models but they had the adulation of the fans. Today's ballplayer is a different breed. A few years ago Jose Cansaco got a 900 telephone number to make a buck off kids phoning to get a taped message of his voice. In 1995, with fans livid over the 1994 strike, Ed Vosberg got caught trying to scalp his complimentary tickets to the all-star game in front of his club the Texas Rangers' home park. These actions don't win the remaining baseball fans to the players' cause.

How many millions of dollars does a guy need to make for playing a kids' game? For me the true essence of baseball is found in the joy of making a difficult running grab or in the thrill of figuring out how to hit a curve ball. It's aspiring to play like a big leaguer no matter how low the level of competition you play against. Johnson and Wolff's *The Encyclopedia of Minor League Baseball* offers ample descriptions of what shoestring glory means. It's William Mack, once a noted minor-league prospect and later a tramp who died of starvation in 1908 in a Pittsburgh hospital. Closer to home there is the tragic tale of Cy Forsythe, a clutch hitter for the Edmonton Eskimos of the Western Canada Baseball League prior to World War I. In 1915 the future looked bright for Forsythe when he signed on with Omaha of the Western League. He left his motherless four-year-old with a couple in Topeka, Kansas, promising his son he would come for him at season's end. When he returned the couple and his child were gone. Forsythe would embark on an eighteen-year search for the boy, one which culminated in a visit to Sacramento Penitentiary where his son languished on death row. The foster father had been a bully who was arrested for passing bad cheques and his destitute wife could not maintain the family home. She took the little boy with her and he was forced to endure a life of hardship that culminated in a murder.

In more recent times it's the sad plight of J. Rodney Richard, formerly of the Houston Astros. Once one of the most feared fireballers in the game, Richard posted over three hundred strikeouts in back-to-back seasons during the late 1970s. In 1980 in the prime of his career, he suffered a paralyzing stroke. Doctors located a blood clot that restricted the blood flow to his brain. Although surgery saved his life, Richard's pitching days were over. He now lives under an expressway in Houston, a troll-like existence which is a far cry from the days when he was "king of the hill" in the Astrodome.

The history of professional baseball on the Canadian Prairies is fraught with failure, occasionally buffered by small victories. Franchises and even leagues have folded with alarming frequency since the turn of this century. The players have run the gamut from future Hall of Famers to brawling hooligans. The crowds have varied from rogues to royalty. These northern climes have forced teams to take the field in snow, gale-force winds, and even an attack of moths, but somehow the game has persevered.

BASEBALL'S ORIGINS AND EARLY GAMES

LIKE MOST CASUAL BASEBALL FANS, I GREW UP BELIEVING THE ABNER Doubleday myth which held that he invented the game and, in 1839, drew up the first playing field at Cooperstown, New York. In fact the latter-day Civil War hero was a second-year student at West Point that year, and nowhere in his voluminous diaries or reminiscences is the game even mentioned.

The main perpetrator of the Doubleday hoax was Albert Spalding, one of baseball's luminaries in the development of the professional game. The first great pitcher of pro ball (he won over two hundred games in the 1870s), Spalding helped found the National League and served as president of the Chicago White Stockings from 1882 to 1891. While still a player in 1876 he started a large baseball emporium to sell baseball equipment, and his annual *Spalding's Official Baseball Guide* was vital in disseminating the rules and records of the game. The Spalding Company branched out into all facets of sport, making its owner a very powerful and respected man. It was vitally important to Spalding that baseball be perceived not only as America's national pastime but also that its origins be seen as purely "stars and stripes." The staunch patriot's nationalistic pride bred an excellent marketing scheme for the game.

In his book *America's National Game* (1911), Spalding refers to baseball as war: "I claim that Base Ball owes its prestige as our National Game to the fact that as no other form of sport it is exponent of American Courage, Confidence, Combativeness; American Dash, Discipline, Determination; American Energy, Eagerness, Enthusiasm; American Pluck, Persistency, Performance; American Spirit, Sagacity, Success; American Vim, Vigor, Virility."

Spalding is less generous when discussing cricket, a sport many believe to be a forerunner to baseball: "Cricket is a splendid game, for Britons. They play Cricket because it accords with the traditions of their country to do so; because it is easy and does not overtax their energy or thought." To him baseball is the perfect democratic game where the swellest of the swell and the humble working man can compete as equals. This equality may have transcended class but not gender: "Base Ball is too strenuous for womankind, except as she may take part in the grandstand, with applause for the brilliant play, with waving kerchief to the hero of the three-bagger, and, since she is ever a loyal partisan of the home team, with smiles of derision for the Umpire when he gives us the worst of it, and, for the same reason, with occasional perfectly decorous demonstrations when it becomes necessary to rattle the opposing pitcher."

In 1907 a commission was formed with a mandate to prove that, despite similarities to earlier ball games like English rounders, baseball was modern and purely American in origin. To this end the committee validated the word of an aging retired mining engineer named Abner Graves who was a boyhood friend of Doubleday and swore that he was present at the alleged first game in 1839. *The Mills Report* written by Abraham G. Mills, third president of the National League and a personal friend of Spalding, carved out Major General Abner Doubleday's place in American mythology.

And what of earlier references to baseball? In his diary Albigence Waldo, a surgeon with Washington's troops at Valley Forge, refers to soldiers batting balls and running bases. Jane Austen mentions the game by name in *Northanger Abbey*, written in the late 1790s and published in 1818. The exploring duo of Lewis and Clark tried to teach the Nez Perce Indians to play the game of base in the early 1800s. Dr. Oliver Wendall Holmes, poet and father of the great American jurist, spoke of playing baseball at Harvard in 1829. These are but a few examples, which do not take into account the ball and stick games like paddle ball, trap ball, one-old cat, and particularly rounders or the game of town ball popular in colonial New England.

Canadians, too, can lay claim to some early form of the game. On June 4, 1838, a contest which included five bases was played in Beechville, Ontario. Wilson Green in his book *Red River Revelations* quotes from a diary written in the 1840s that discusses a game called "bat." The contest was played amongst the older boys of the settlement and often led to fisticuffs. In *Women of Red River*, W. J. Healy tells of Mrs. Neil Campbell making leather balls for the boys to use in the playing of "bat and ball."

In the mid-nineteenth century baseball appeared to be a regional phenomenon, with different areas applying their own sets of rules to the game. The Canadian Game played in southwestern Ontario had five bases and eleven players; in order to put a side out and earn a turn at bat, all eleven players had to be retired. Suffice to say this made for some high-scoring affairs.

Albert Spalding's criticism of cricket did not give the British import its due. Baseball owes much of its terminology to cricket; terms like "innings" and "umpires" are borrowed from the British import. Henry Chadwick, deemed the founding father of baseball reporting, laced his column with cricket phrases like "batsmen," "playing for the side," and "excellent field." William Harry Wright, another pioneer of the diamond and the man recognized as the father of professional baseball, was a former professional cricket player and later a successful manager. Wright applied his vast knowledge of cricket in promoting baseball as a team sport.

Played from the 1840s to the outbreak of the Civil War, the

Massachusetts Game was a popular variation on baseball. The contest was played on an irregular four-sided field enclosing four bases set at asymmetrical distances from one another, with the striker or batter positioned away from home plate. A team was permitted ten to fourteen "scouts" or fielders, and only one out had to be recorded to end an inning. Fielders could put a batter out by catching the ball on the fly or on one bounce. A player could also be retired if he was hit by a thrown ball while running the base path. This practice was called "soaking the runner."

With the introduction of the New York Game by the Knickerbocker Club in 1845, baseball took a big step toward its present form. While not as gentrified as the members of the rival New York Athletic Club, the Knickerbockers viewed the game as the pursuit of gentlemen, and wanted matches to be contested on a strictly amateur basis. One of their members, Alexander Cartwright, designed a diamond-shaped field and set the bases ninety feet apart. Standing only forty-five feet away from the batter, the pitcher threw the ball in a stiff-armed, underhand fashion. This variation on the game introduced the "three strikes and you're out" rule. Outs were recorded by catching the ball on the fly or on one bounce, and a runner could be retired by throwing a fielded ball to first base ahead of the batter. Cartwright's rules included the contemporary standard of three outs per inning and called for nine players on the field per team.

The "Knicks" honed their skills at Madison Square, located between 23rd and 26th Streets along Madison Avenue in Manhattan. In 1846 the Knickerbockers played the first game employing Cartwright's rules at Elysian Fields, in Hoboken, New Jersey, a popular weekend spot for working-class families. The area was perceived as vulgar by New York's elite, who attempted to pattern their leisure time after the English aristocracy. The Elysian Fields were typical of the amusement parks of the time, housing a gaming house, drinking saloon, and billiard room. These common touches appalled the upper crust of Gotham, who sought the isolation of their own social strata.

Historian David Voight has done extensive research into the backgrounds of the members of the Knickerbocker Club roster between 1845 and 1860. He feels that the membership catered to gentlemen wannabes, with clerks, merchants, a "segar dealer," a hatter, a stationer, and a U.S. marshal. Alexander Cartwright, the man responsible for drafting the rules of play, was a fireman.

The New York Game was rapidly adopted by the other fledgling ball clubs in New York. In keeping with their tradition as innovators, the Knickerbockers introduced the first team uniforms on June 3, 1851, with attire that included straw hats, blue full-length trousers, and white shirts. Baseball may have been a regional phenomenon with strong support situated in the northern and midwestern states, but New York was the game's Mecca. By the 1850s there was scarcely a spare blade of grass in a ten-mile radius of the city that was not being turned into a playing field. The game's alarming popularity led to the inception of clubs complete with clubhouses, playing fields, and the prerequisite hierarchy of officers. Since there were no formal leagues it was incumbent upon the club secretary to arrange contests. Everyone vied for a shot at the vaunted Knickerbockers, but they often eschewed challenges and played amongst themselves or, when they saw fit, accepted a match with some other suitably genteel club like the Excelsior Club of Brooklyn. Although reluctant to display their superiority on the playing field, the Knickerbockers wanted pre-eminence over all the upstart clubs and insisted that the game remain the domain of gentlemen.

However, the new sports juggernaut could not be harnessed, and by the end of the decade competition had supplanted recreation. Clubs were ever on the lookout for more talented players, with an eye toward victories and gate receipts, not merely a social outing.

In 1858 the Knickerbockers' reign would be usurped by the National Association of Base Ball Players when twenty-five clubs united to standardize the rules and set out guidelines for team competition. The Association established the nine-inning duration and the pitcher's box and also sanctioned the charging of admission. Fifteen hundred enthusiasts parted with fifty cents to watch the Brooklyn and New York All-Star teams clash that year. Two years later the Association could boast a roster of sixty teams with representatives from the East, Midwest, and some college clubs.

In 1860 a three-game series was played between the Brooklyn Excelsiors and a decidedly more rough-around-the-edges Atlantic Club. This working-class men's club boasted over two hundred members and had strong ties with the local Democratic party. The Atlantics tried to maintain some semblance of decorum while on the playing field but their supporters were not above booing the opposition or the umpire. Ted Vincent in *The Rise and Fall of American Sports* chronicles a contest that attracted enough pickpockets to inspire an anti-pickpocket riot.

The Excelsiors had been defeated by the Atlantics in a contest two years earlier, in which the victors gloated, saying that they were the better-conditioned nine, owing to their outdoor jobs. The Brooklyn club did not want to risk another humiliating defeat and signed James Creighton, the leading hurler of the time, to its roster. Unknown to its rivals Creighton was being paid for his services, making him the game's first professional. He was well worth the money in the opening contest of the series, shutting down the Atlantic bats in a 23-4 victory before more than ten thousand spectators. Creighton was ill and could not pitch in the second game. This time over twelve thousand fans were on hand, along with seventy of New York's finest to keep order. The Atlantics prevailed 15-14 but the police were placed on alert when "a gang of toughs" bragged that they would not allow the Excelsiors a victory in the deciding encounter. The crowd was estimated at between fifteen and twenty thousand for the finale, with a strong police presence to prevent any trouble. The Excelsiors led 8-4 going into the bottom of the fifth inning but the Atlantics scored two runs and threatened to make a game of it. A close play at third ended the inning. Although reports of the time claimed that the Atlantic runner overran the bag and was tagged out, the call did not sit well with the team's supporters. There were vocal demands for the umpire's resignation, something that contravened all notions of a gentlemen's competition. The crowd became more unruly when a close call went in favour of the Excelsiors in the top of the sixth. Ultimately it was an error by an Atlantic player that pushed that team's supporters over the limit. The police were sent into the crowd to try and restore order. When this proved to no avail, the Excelsiors walked off the field. This marked the end of baseball as a polite game.

By 1862 the first enclosed park was established in New York by an entrepreneur named William Cammeyer. His principal tenant was not one of the game's genteel practitioners but ward-boss "Big Jim" Tweed's Mutuals.

No one event did more to spread baseball's popularity than the Civil War. In *Total Baseball*, David Voight identifies the east-west alignment of the game's professional franchises as a legacy of the war between the states. It would be 1962, almost a century after the war ended, before the Houston Colt 45s would become the first major-league franchise south of the Mason Dixon Line. By the end of the Civil War baseball was a known commodity in every state to which Union soldiers returned.

By 1867 the Association's rolls had swelled to include three hundred clubs, with more than one-third coming from the Midwest. The Washington Nationals embarked on a tour and suffered their lone defeat at the hands of the Rockford, Illinois, Forest City nine and their fine young pitcher Al Spalding. The success of the Nationals' tour only heightened the need for an organized league with a fixed schedule. Further rule changes in the 1860s helped to streamline the game and make it more competitive: the one bounce for an out was eliminated, and players took to leaving their feet and sliding to avoid being tagged on the base paths. With the development of Arthur "Candy" Cummings' wrist-twisting motion, perfected while skipping clam shells on a New England beach, the "curve" ball was born. At five foot nine inches and 120 pounds, Cummings was one of the Association's first stars during his five-year career from 1872 to 1877. Significant improvement was made in fielding as well as in pitching during this period.

The sheer popularity of baseball contrived to undermine the Association's grip on the game. As more clubs began to charge admission, the players as the providers of the entertainment wanted to share in the revenue. Although this created a class of professional ballplayers that threatened the mandate of amateurism inherent in the National Association of Base Ball Players code, the organization did nothing to stem the tide toward professionalism. Instead it went so far as to define what constituted a pro. Anyone receiving a share of gate receipts or who held a job solely on his ability to play ball was no longer considered an amateur. What strikes a familiar note with today's game is that players considered themselves free agents, capable of going to the highest bidder whenever it suited them. This type of player was called a "revolver," one who posed a serious threat to the Association's authority.

As baseball evolved from the Knickerbocker ideal of gentlemen's recreation into a business, a man's skill on a ball diamond could now provide him with a livelihood. Writing in 1868, the dean of baseball scribes, Henry Chadwick, used the Brooklyn Atlantics club to illustrate the new hierarchy that the game was taking on. A club could carry up to three nines in its organization: the professional team held the place of honour, followed by the competitive amateur team; of the least consequence to the club were those members known derisively as "muffins" who merely played the game for fun. A club might finance its professional team through selling stock shares or relying solely on gate receipts.

The debate over professionalism remained covert until 1869 when the Cincinnati Red Stockings announced their intention of fielding a fully salaried team. While hardly the first professional team, Cincinnati was the first to declare itself so, and led by player-manager Harry Wright, the Red Stockings embarked on a tour of the United States, going sixty games without a loss. Thanks to Wright, they were far better at the game's fundamentals than any of their opponents. Wright had invented the fundamentals, having the club take batting practice and infield and outfield practice, and working on cutoff throws. Unfortunately the team's success on the field did not translate into profit for its backers, and the club reverted to amateurism the following year. However, by calling themselves professionals, Cincinnati brought the amateur versus professional conflict to a head, and in 1870, when the National Association attempted to return the game to a strictly amateur status, the professional delegates walked out. In March of 1871, they started their own organization with the inception of the National Association of Professional Baseball Players.

Despite the wealth of evidence to refute American claims to inventing the game, the United States can certainly claim to be an innovator in baseball. Cartwright's New York Game did not reach Canada until 1859 and was adopted in the first match between rival clubs played in this country. The contest saw the Toronto Young Canadians outlast the Hamilton Young Americans 68-41 in a slugfest. The affair was marred

by poor fielding, no doubt owing to the lack of ball gloves and the fact that the batter could designate where he wanted the ball pitched. In 1872 an Ottawa-based club imported two American players, and the following year, the Guelph Maple Leafs added two American pros to their already formidable line-up. Two years later the Maple Leafs captured the World Semi-Professional Baseball Championship in Watertown, New York, with a roster laced with American professionals. In 1875 the London Tucumsehs, a Canadian-based team comprised exclusively of American players, defeated the American champion Chicago White Stockings 4-3, no mean feat as Chicago boasted the two dominant players of the time, Albert Spalding and Cap Anson, in its line-up. The next season London took the measure of the Pittsburgh Alleghenies to win the International Association championship.

While Doubleday and Cooperstown are not the true origins of baseball, the United States refined and popularized the game into what it is today. Canada can certainly claim its share of outstanding ballplayers in the game's formative years. Writing at the turn of the century, J. P. Fitzgerald of Toronto listed Arthur Irwin, Tip O'Neill, Bob Emslie, and Dr. Peter Wood as pioneers in the early American pro leagues. Even Spalding did not refute the claim that Canadians were becoming increasingly proficient at the game. Nevertheless he credited such proficiency to the fact that Canadians, while British by origin, had absorbed Yankee "know how" from being in commercial competition with American businessmen. He further held that it was British opposition to professionalism that limited the Canadian game, and urged that fit and capable young players seek employment in the United States.

BASEBALL COMES
TO THE PRAIRIES

MANITOBA ENTERED INTO CONFEDERATION IN 1870; THREE YEARS LATER, ON November 8, the City of Winnipeg was incorporated. It is probable that the revised game of baseball was brought to Winnipeg through the influx of settlers from eastern Canada or contact with the Red River Settlement's major trading centre in St. Paul. On March 18, 1874, a group of men met at the Davis Hotel to organize the first baseball club. That day thirty members including an executive enlisted, to be followed by more enthusiasts.

The Winnipeg club must have patterned itself after the Knicker-bocker model as recreation for gentlemen. Most of its participants were wealthy. The club executive reads like a Who's Who of early Manitoba society. The stately Main Street residence (dubbed the Bannatyne Castle) of club president A. G. Bannatyne, a wealthy merchant and the city's first postmaster, had held the first meeting of the Manitoba Legislature. H. G. McMicken, one of the club's vice-presidents, established the Dominion Land Office in the city, while another V.P., Arthur Higgins, was a partner in the successful Higgins and Young importers' firm.

It is interesting to note that the founding of this organization predates the establishment of curling and cricket clubs, long perceived as more popular pastimes. In that the rigours of prairie life left little time for recreation, there are scant references to sport of any variety in the first few years of the *Manitoba Free Press*. Dominion and Arbour days are the rare exception when mention is made of games and footraces; and line scores occasionally appear for cricket matches between teams from Headingley, Selkirk, or the military. The first reference to horse racing at the Turf Club appears in 1876, and the lawyers take on a team of local bankers in a cricket match that same year.

On July 3, 1877, the *Manitoba Free Press* chronicled a ball game pitting a club known as the Stars against the importing firm of Higgins, Young, and Jackson. The game, held in conjunction with Dominion Day festivities, offers interesting insight into early sports reporting. The article discusses the team uniforms in elaborate detail. It was readily apparent that the Stars were the better team as the importers were limited to fielding a squad from the ranks of their employ. As many of the HY&J nine had only played ball a couple of times, their fielding left a great deal to be desired. The local scribe had this to say about the Stars:

> The Stars twinkled brightly, and in the constellation were a number of crack players. Whether at bat or in the field the nine showed to great advantage. Their play at times reminded one of professionals, and notwithstanding that their club is a new one, the activity in fielding and precision in throwing clearly demonstrated that in the ranks were "veterans of the diamond."

The Stars may have thrashed their opponents by a score of 77-4 but this did not prevent the two clubs from retiring to McCaskill's restaurant where a bountiful table of food was provided by the losers.

P. G. Laurie started the bi-weekly *Saskatchewan Herald,* published out of Battleford in the territory of Assiniboia, in 1878. For the August 11, 1879 issue a correspondent dispatched a description of a contest played in Prince Albert where the town divided itself into those living above and below the local mission. The Lower Mission side prevailed 45-32. Interest was such that a club was formed, with Sub-Constable Robertson as captain. The first order on the agenda was to send away for bats, balls, and a copy of the rules of the game.

Dominion Day 1880 in Winnipeg saw a return to the diamond as the Poplar Leaf club prepared to battle the Athletic Club in a match billed as the Provincial Championship. The game was to be played at Dufferin Park, the city's first real sports facility, but the wide variety of other activities limited the crowd at the ball field. The *Free Press* conceded the clear superiority of the Poplar Leaf side but praised the fielding of the Athletics' Dick and Van Vliet as well as the officiating. "Mr. S. J. Van Rensselaer umpired with his usual urbanity and even handed justice and his decisions gave the utmost satisfaction to both clubs. The game was remarkable for the good feeling manifested by the contestants."

During the early 1880s baseball appears to have taken a downturn on the Prairies. Press coverage is given to cricket, lacrosse, horse racing, and rowing, with scant mention of ball. The *Herald* did cover a contest played at celebrations for the queen's birthday in 1881 when the Battleford Northwest Mounted Police detachment took on a team of local citizens. This time the Mounties did not get their man, for the locals prevailed 29-13.

In July 1885 at Dufferin Park the Winnipeg Baseball Club played a game against the Halifax Battalion, with Isaac Pitblado, whose legal career spanned six decades in Winnipeg, patrolling centre field. Lawyers were also front and centre when the first game of baseball was played in Brandon that October. The town lawyers and bankers banded together to take on all comers and managed to squeak out a 197-180 victory. There was a hung jury on the results as umpire A. C. Fraser had based many of his decisions on a lacrosse manual. Thomas Mayne Daly, the first juvenile court judge in Manitoba, amused the spectators with his sky-wiping at the plate, while lawyer MacDonald's somersault on the base path resulted in ripped trousers.

Novelty sports were all the rage in Brandon at that time. Baseball was played on roller skates with comic results, and cyclists often raced roller skaters, with "punters" placing wagers on the outcome.

Sports truly came of age on the Prairies with the completion of the C.P.R. line in 1885 and the subsequent opening of the West. By 1886 the *Manitoba Free Press* featured a sports and pastimes column which covered American professional baseball for the first time on the Prairies. With baseball's increased popularity came the founding of a new Manitoba League. The circuit included three Winnipeg clubs – the Hotels, the Metropolitans, and the C.P.R. – and a squad from Portage la Prairie. Much to the chagrin of their competitors the Metropolitans dipped into the professional ranks by signing pitcher J. Young and his battery-mate J. R. Barnfather from a club in Hamilton. The Hotels

"The Marvellous Mets"
The 1886 Winnipeg Metropolitans, runners-up in the
first professional league on the Prairies.

quickly followed suit in the signing of their own battery of Prescott and Milbourn from Minneapolis.

The league opener between the "Mets" and C.P.R. was awaited with great anticipation as it would mark the debut of a calibre of baseball not yet seen in Winnipeg. Of the crowd of fifteen hundred supporters that flocked to Dufferin Park, few were disappointed in the first-rate performance they witnessed. Gambling was prevalent at all sporting events and the Mets were a two-to-one favourite to carry the day. A. W. Paulin, a former member of the Ontario club Harriston Brownstocking, was on the mound for the railway club, while the Hamilton professional Young took the hill for the Mets. It didn't take the C.P.R. hitters long to figure out Young's delivery and they hit his pitches freely, but his battery-mate Barnfather impressed the fans with his quick bat and fine defence behind the plate. The railway nine's superior hitting and fielding led them to a 7-4 triumph in what was considered the finest game ever witnessed in Winnipeg. The *Free Press* applauded both sides for "a noticeable absence of anything pertaining to rudeness."

Could this stellar start to the campaign be maintained? Unfortunately, for financial reasons, the Portage la Prairie club had to bow out of the league after playing only one game. But the influx of professional talent continued to stock the three remaining teams and by mid-July fifteen American pro ballplayers had made their way to Winnipeg. The league was becoming so competitive that the Mets took to advertising in the southern Ontario newspapers.

Even a lowly circuit like the Manitoba League was not exempt from a "revolver" controversy as players tried to make the best deal possible for themselves. The Mets promptly withdrew from the league over a conflict with the C.P.R. stemming from a dispute about a player named Mackenzie who had originally come to Winnipeg as the property of the Hotels team. Mackenzie would later tell a tribunal that he had made a verbal commitment to A. W. Paulin of the C.P.R. team as part of a stipulation for garnering his release from the Hotels. The Hotels were interested in preventing Mackenzie from joining their chief rivals, the Metropolitans, but no sooner had he procured his release than he signed a contract with them. A. W. Paulin was furious when Mackenzie took the field for the Mets against his club in a game at Selkirk on July 28, 1886, and demanded the contest be annulled. The Metropolitans refused, and they quit the league to voice their displeasure. After two weeks in limbo they returned without Mackenzie, who was subsequently banned from the Manitoba League.

Unable to put aside such petty squabbling, the league limped through its first season. A contest between the two front-runners in August illustrated that the teams would resort to devious methods to attain victory. Hotel third baseman James Cantillion twice fell in front of Metropolitan base runners, tripping them as they ran for home plate. The *Free Press* reported that a significant sum of money changed hands in betting circles during the Hotels' 14-8 triumph. Since Met pitcher Young had a particularly poor outing (including two errant throws to first), suspicions were cast on his integrity. The Metropolitan management contacted the press to exonerate their player and offered a reward of one hundred dollars to anyone who could prove skulduggery on the pitcher's part.

The Manitoba League was suffering from more than its share of growing pains but it was the C.P.R. club's decision to disband in

September 1886 that sounded the death knell for the circuit. Meeting at the Nickel Plate Hotel on September 2, the team decided to terminate its affairs after paying off all its players in full. A prominent team member told the press that they had entered the league without foreseeing the introduction of professionals. They believed then and continued to think that their club was the best amateur nine in the Northwest. The team had remained solely amateur until July 1, and when they did begin importing professionals, it led to financial difficulties. The league plodded through the final month of the season with only two teams; the Winnipeg Hotels captured the inaugural and only Manitoba League championship.

"Take Me Out to the Ball Game"
An undated contest in the Qu'Appelle Valley.
Future premier Walter Scott on the mound.

There is no mention of baseball in the *Saskatchewan Herald* in 1886 but cricket matches and rifle-range contests are reported in the newpaper's new weekly format. The next season a Regina-based club with the redoubtable pitcher Walter Scott toured the territory by train, accepting all challenges. The club went on to capture the Silver Cup, emblematic of the area's top team, but plans to organize a territorial championship had to be scrapped due to a lack of entrants. Walter Scott's life would be equally eventful away from the diamond. He purchased a newspaper called the *Leader* in 1895 and, ten years later, would be the province of Saskatchewan's first premier, a position he held for twelve years.

Baseball was slow to gain acceptance in Saskatchewan. The 1889 Victoria Day contest between the Mounted Police detachment and local citizens had to be cancelled because of a lack of interest. The game fared slightly better in Alberta, where the *Lethbridge News* covered a Dominion Day contest between teams from Medicine Hat and Lethbridge. A local reporter described the game as the highlight of the festivities, with many people making the trip to Lethbridge for the sole purpose of witnessing the contest. Lethbridge supporters offered even money on their boys but there were few takers. The Lethbridge side prevailed 17-9, forcing one female Medicine Hat rooter to complain that they were cheating by not throwing the ball so the visitors could hit it. The correspondent reserved high praise for the new Lethbridge catcher Hansen: "The man who holds 'Bob's' delivery wants a cool head, a quick eye and plenty of nerve. Stay with it, Charley, we all like your grit."

The Queen City Champs, the Regina Baseball Team, 1888
Back row: C. Willoughby, catcher; E. McCarthy, first base; Shellington, centre field; Walter Scott, pitcher. Middle row: Hamilton, president; J.W. Smith, vice-president. Front row: R. Sweet, left field; W. Bole, second base; R.B. Ferguson, shortstop; J.C. Pope, third base; J. McLaughlin, right field.

"Never Let Your Opponent See You Smile"
The Moosomin Girl's Baseball Team, 1905.

Women began playing baseball at the American women's college Vassar in 1865. By the mid-1880s working-class women formed barnstorming teams. The first female touring clubs drew mainly negative press that stressed the unfeminine nature of the players and editorialized that no self-respecting girl would take up the game. Even in Saskatchewan the joys of the diamond were not a strictly male domain when women took to the field at the Dominion Day picnic at Regina in 1891. Nine years later some city fathers were appalled by the spectacle of the touring "Boston Bloomer Girls." This term was often a misnomer since most of the touring Bloomer teams had male participants. The troupe touring the Prairies had a male catcher and first-sacker. It got the better of an all-male team from Moose Jaw before being threatened with a protest by some of the more conservative city fathers in Regina. In the end the spirit of competition prevailed and the Bloomers edged a Regina nine with a strong Mountie presence 13-12. At the turn of the century there were touring Bloomer troupes from Kansas City, New York and Texas whose alumni included the likes of the great pitcher "Smokey Joe" Wood and Rogers Hornsby, both future major-league stars.

In the truest sense professional baseball did not return to the Prairies

"On the Road Again"
The Namao Ladies' Hardball Team at Morinville, Alberta, circa 1920.

in the nineteenth century. However, where games were matters of civic pride there was a fine brand of ball being played in western Manitoba towns. In 1893 E. H. Garrison had organized a fine ball club in Virden, and five years later it formed a league with Souris and Brandon. The Virden team imported a battery from Guelph to face Brandon in the season-ending Labour Day series. Brandon must have gotten wind of the imports, for on game day it took the field with three of its own Guelph imports and two players from Toronto.

In the autumn of 1898 the Virden club went on to play in the Provincial Championship in Winnipeg. Baseball's popularity was languishing at that time, and so the Virden nine netted a paltry $9.50 for two contests held at Fort Garry Park. The few fans who witnessed Virden's triumph in both games agreed that it was the finest baseball seen in the city since the disbanding of the Manitoba League.

By far the most competitive team in Manitoba, the Virden club continued its winning ways in 1901, capturing its own tournament. The club then travelled to Winnipeg for a four-game series with the Winnipeg Unions but could only manage a split. Bill Orr lost the final game 9-5 for the lone defeat that he would suffer in Manitoba that year. A local reporter attributed the long-term success of Virden to team harmony: a player could make an error without fear of being lambasted by his mates and there were no cliques in the club.

Just how seriously was baseball taken in western Manitoba? In 1903 Brandon joined Virden and Portage la Prairie in the short-lived Manitoba Senior League. The club's battery of George Doucette and Ed McCarthy was lionized in the rural town. When the league disbanded after a single season, both men were picked up by major-league organizations.

Baseball was not an instant success in an era driven by an agrarian economy that embraced long hours and hard physical labour. However, the Prairies were being populated at an astounding rate at the turn of the century as Britain poured money into developing the Canadian West. The economic boom of the first decade of this century awakened an entrepreneurial spirit among some sportsmen, and the business of baseball beckoned.

"Play Ball"
The fans await the start of a game at Regina's Railway Park in 1903.

FOUL WHISKY BREATH

THE HISTORY OF PROFESSIONAL BASEBALL ON THE PRAIRIES CAN EASILY BE divided between that of the unaffiliated minor-league era prior to World War II and the current major-league farm-team system. Manitoba was the first Prairie province to return to the pro game when the Winnipeg Maroons entered the newly formed Northern League in 1902. The club was owned by R. J. Smith, a representative of the Great Northern Railway, who envisioned running train excursions filled with local supporters between Winnipeg and its league rivals in North Dakota and Minnesota. While Winnipeggers flocked to take the "weekend specials" out to Lake Winnipeg or Minaki Lodge in Ontario, the excursions of "bleacher bums" to American towns like Fargo and Grand Forks never did materialize. However, the Maroons were the lynchpin of the "polar circuit," often drawing upwards of four thousand fans out to their home field at River Park. This was Class D ball, the lowest rung on the minor-league ladder. With every winning streak or surge at the turnstiles, the local press would cite some unnamed source promising Winnipeg's entry into a better circuit the following season.

   This was a simpler time when the public still viewed some athletes as local heroes. Arthur Marcan, the Maroons' second baseman in their

"We Are the Champions"
Winnipeg Maroons, the 1907 Northern Copper Baseball League champions.

inaugural season, could have stepped out of a Frank Capra movie script. He didn't smoke, chew tobacco, or drink, and was constantly training; in fact when he left his home town of Wausau, Wisconsin, to come to Winnipeg, the local townspeople gave him a rousing send-off at the train station. Young Marcan lived up to his advance billing with a solid

Action from River Park, 1907.

campaign that saw him promoted to St. Paul of the American Association by season's end. Twenty years later, when his playing career ended, Marcan returned to the Prairies as a popular umpire in the Western Canada League.

The Western Canada League (W.C.L.) began in Alberta in 1907 with teams in Edmonton, Calgary, Medicine Hat, and Lethbridge. Two years later the league doubled its franchises with the addition of Moose Jaw, Regina, Brandon, and Winnipeg. Like the Northern League this was Class D ball, paying low wages and often attracting some very rough customers. The local accounts of the day are filled with stories of players and managers being assessed five-dollar fines for their abuse of umpires.

"Winter Ball!"
In Alberta, Lethbridge plays Calgary on January 27, 1906.

In several instances the abuse was more than just verbal. In a contest played in June 1907 two Lethbridge players were fined twenty-five dollars apiece for attacking an umpire. The Miners' pitcher Klippert became so incensed over a game against Medicine Hat not being called for darkness that he threw a ball at the umpire, striking him squarely in the back. To compound the indignity, Lethbridge's shortstop Egan punched the beleaguered official in the face. This outburst gave the game to Medicine Hat, one of the Hatters' many triumphs on the road to the initial league championship.

By 1909 the expanded W.C.L. was attempting to promote professional baseball across the Prairies, and the owners of the league, possessing a wisdom that far outstrips that of the current brain trust in the majors, imposed profit-sharing. The league threatened a suit against the Winnipeg City Council when it learned that the Barnum Circus would take over Happylands, the Maroons' home field, for the all-important Dominion Day holiday. The circuit could ill afford the loss of a gate receipt from its largest franchise. As in all business partnerships, tempers flared when the crowds fell off. Edmonton club president Frank Gray accused the Maroons of being four-flushers who padded their home attendance while looking down their noses at the other W.C.L. franchises. He wondered where all the fans disappeared to when his Eskimos played in the "Chicago of the North." Gray told reporters that his club was lucky to make expenses during a stopover in Winnipeg and hoped that Edmonton fans would show the Maroons the same lack of support when they travelled to the Alberta capital.

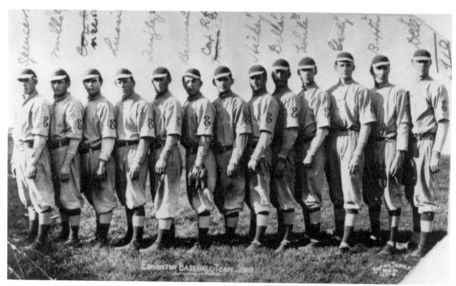

"The Starting Line-up"
The Edmonton Eskimos 1910 squad.

Fortunately not all the news from the W.C.L. revolved around brawling and bickering. The newspapers occasionally carried a humorous story. On September 3, 1909, the *Winnipeg Tribune* was having difficulty covering a contest between the Maroons and the Brandon Angels. The regular sports reporter was out with a voluptuous toothache, leaving the assignment up for grabs. Both the proofreader and the printer's devil lobbied hard for an afternoon in the fresh air but it was ultimately decided that nine staff members would each take an inning. The society editor took the first inning and filed this report:

> The sun spread its transcendent rays over a field that was beautifully green and there was not the slightest trace of cloud to mar the almost perfect afternoon; consequently a large and fashionable audience was present to view the interesting proceedings.
>
> Notwithstanding the extreme heat, many wore their new fall hats and the scene was one of unusual brilliance, forming a kaleidscope [sic] picture that would have done credit to any comedic opera setting. That the new styles are going to be popular was fully brought to light by the fact that so many new hats were being worn so early in the season.
>
> One lady, who was becoming in a pink creation, of the latest mode, and relieved by unique flounces, wore one of the latest imported hats which made a charming effect, giving her the appearance of a ballroom belle.

When the Angels were set down in order in the top of the first inning, the society editor had this to say of the Maroons' lead-off hitter:

> Mr. Laurence Piper was the debutante, and his coming out was highly successful from an artistic point of view. Like his teammates Mr. Piper was bedecked in a rich maroon costume. His hair [was] parted in the middle and his general deportment [was] of fitting modesty.

Incidents of bad behaviour were not limited to the playing field alone. That volatile combination of whisky and wagers often led to some deplorable conduct in the stands. A comment in the *Winnipeg Tribune* in 1910 notes, "As long as a male fan is allowed to blow foul whiskey breath in a lady's face, women should be encouraged to wear a 'Merry Widow' hat to the ball park."

While players' temper tantrums, drunken fans, and gambling may have been the more prevalent ills associated with Prairie ball, racism was by no means a purely American phenomenon. Black ballplayers had been banished from the American professional leagues since the 1890s. In 1887 black players were openly ridiculed in the *Hamilton Spectator*, and Torontonians chanted "kill the nigger" when Frank Grant took the field for Buffalo the same year. In 1910 the Western Canada League had

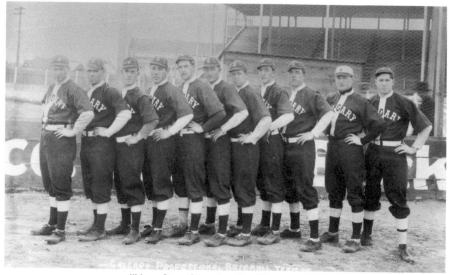

"Hey, Stop Standing So Close to Me"
The Calgary Broncos Baseball Club, 1910.

its own racist incident when Medicine Hat refused to take the field in
Regina if the Bonepilers' third baseman Brookins was not removed from
the game. Dick Brookins had been signed out of St. Louis, purporting to
be of native American extraction. Early in the season both Calgary and
Medicine Hat lodged protests on the grounds of the player's negroid
features. The matter was referred to the National Commission of Baseball for a ruling, and its findings concluded that Brookins' family came
from an exclusively white neighbourhood in St. Louis. However, W.C.L.
president Eckstrom chose to disregard the commission's findings and
branded Brookins an "alleged negro," banishing him from further play
in the W.C.L. Regina's manager Walters stood his ground and refused to
remove his third-sacker, losing the contest to forfeit and being threatened with a fifty-dollar fine for his attempt at a civil-rights stand.

Class D was either the starting-point or the ultimate descent for a
professional career. For John C. Bender, brother of the legendary Yankee
hurler Albert "Chief" Bender, it fell into the latter category when he
toiled for the Edmonton Eskimos in 1911. Three years earlier, while
playing for Columbus, Bender had stabbed his manager Win Clark
during an altercation on a steamer bound from Jacksonville to
Charleston. Bender had served a two-year suspension from pro ball and

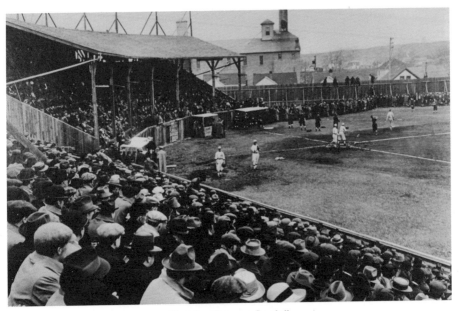

"Let the Season Begin"
Fans pack Diamond Park in Edmonton for the 1910 home
opener between the Eskimos and Saskatoon Quakers.

was trying to revive what was left of his career when he dropped dead of a heart attack at Edmonton's Diamond Park.

The 1913 campaign established a new low for rowdiness both on the field and in the stands. League officials began to fear for their personal safety as bench jockeying took on a more threatening dimension. The Saskatoon Quakers, for example, had a talented but ornery ball club that took delight in making an umpire's life miserable. Their fiery shortstop Chick needed a police escort to force him from the playing field after a heated debate with an umpire in Medicine Hat. Poor umpire Taylor had an even worse encounter with some irate fans at Diamond Park in Edmonton. An angry mob surrounded the diamond after the contest; luckily for him, former Gray Bird president and current league president Frank W. Gray was in attendance and spirited the terrified official off the premises. Umpire MacDonald needed the support of some of Saskatoon's finest to make it to his car after a game. Even the police presence did not prevent one lunatic from making a lunge for the ump. The officers subdued the culprit only to be bullied into releasing him by the mob.

True to form, it was umpiring disputes that took centre stage in the league championship between the Moose Jaw Robin Hoods and the Saskatoon Quakers in 1913. The Quakers were at their belligerent best during the series, in no way endearing themselves to umpire Dyer. One Saskatoon player had even stooped to spitting on the man in blue. Moose Jaw led the series three games to two as the clubs battled in a tight pitchers' duel in the sixth game. The Quakers pushed across two runs in the top of the ninth inning to take a 3-2 lead. It was at this point that Dyer chose to exact his revenge. Glancing skyward at a sun far from setting, he decided to call the game for darkness. This meant that the score would revert to the last completed inning, giving the game and the series to Moose Jaw. The league office in Edmonton was inundated with calls of protest from Saskatoon. The Quakers demanded the sixth game as a victory or on a forfeit. The league waffled before finally deciding that the game should be replayed at the neutral site of Regina. This solution was deemed unacceptable by both clubs, and the league took the unusual step of declaring joint winners that season.

In 1914 the W.C.L. owners felt that they had turned the corner and were on the road to stability and profit. The season opened on an optimistic note when Edmonton began its season with a league-record crowd of forty-three hundred fans. But the Albertans had little time to savour their accomplishment because J. F. Cairns, a Saskatoon business-man, had just spent twelve thousand dollars on a new ballpark for the Quakers. Cairns' investment paid immediate dividends when a throng of sixty-five hundred vocal supporters cheered their hometown heroes on to a 6-4 triumph over provincial rival Regina.

Sadly there is more to life than chasing a ball. Canada's entry into World War I left Prairie residents with more pressing matters to occupy their time. Crowds diminished steadily throughout the summer until it became impossible for the home team to assure the visiting club of a sixty-dollar guarantee. In August the league disbanded to prevent club owners' further financial hardships. League-leading Saskatoon was declared the pennant winner.

The situation was entirely different for the Winnipeg Maroons, who had returned to the Northern League in 1913. All the clubs in the polar circuit with the exception of Winnipeg and Fort William were based in American cities. In fact the ever-present rumours of bigger and better

"Give em Hell, Boys"
The 1917 Great War Baseball Champions at Hastings, England.

things permeate the sports pages of the time. A story that appeared in the *Manitoba Free Press* on July 31 suggests that the league was not spending all of its profits on the essentials of the game. The Maroons were playing Winona in a tight contest at Winnipeg's River Park. The home team had snapped a two-all deadlock with a pair of runs in the bottom of the eighth inning, taking the field for the top of the ninth; but the game ball was strangely missing in action. Umpire Ted Flood had already exhausted his supply of game balls and gave Winona one minute to produce *the* ball. Winona's first-sacker De Rusha had been the last player to handle the baseball when he recorded the third out of the previous inning. The visiting team played dumb, claiming no responsibility, and ultimately suffered a 9-0 loss by default.

Ballplayers were a transitory lot in the early days and not beyond resorting to a little trickery when it suited their purposes. Winnipeg owner Charlie Moll was stung by a bogus batsman during the 1916 season. The Maroons were courting a player named Shannon with a reputation as a proven professional in the eastern United States. Negotiations reached the stage where Moll sent the player a one-way ticket to Winnipeg for a tryout. Moll was confident enough in the man's credentials to offer a few of Winnipeg's spare players to other clubs in the Northern League that were beginning to experience difficulty in filling their rosters. When Shannon failed to materialize, Moll prepared to file a grievance with the National Association of Baseball Clubs to have the player blacklisted. Just prior to his lodging the complaint a man purporting to be Shannon arrived in town. It was too late to hold the tryout in Winnipeg so Maroon manager Jack Sheehan took the player on the road to Fargo, planning to utilize his new recruit during the road trip. Sheehan was in for a rude awakening when Shannon took batting practice in Fargo. The man could not hit a lick. Worse, he was a positive liability in the outfield. After witnessing the hapless fielder play several balls off his head, Sheehan called the man in, firing him on the spot. When Moll got word of the flagrant hoodwinking, he filed a formal complaint against the real Shannon.

The Maroons won the pennant that season, paced by their slugging centre-fielder Hack Miller. Miller was good enough to have been given a tryout with the Brooklyn Dodgers the previous season. Feasting on Northern League pitching, he topped the circuit with a .335 batting average and ten round-trippers. Baseball is a statistician's dream but even a rotisserie-league fanatic like myself was astounded to read about one feat that Miller recorded. On June 19, 1916, Hack hit a fungo 438½ feet for a new world record, bettering Ed Walsh's old mark by nineteen feet.

"Bring Your Bathing Suit, It's a Double-header"
The Norwood Ball Park under water during the spring flood of 1916.

"Dropping Off the First Ball"
World War I ace "Wop" May drops off the first baseball for
the season opener of 1919 at Edmonton's Diamond Park.

Winnipeg and Fargo met in the league championship series that season. The Maroons captured the first three contests in the chippy series despite losing their manager-shortstop Sheehan to a broken leg in a collision at the plate in the second game. All that remained was one more road victory for Winnipeg to claim its first league championship since 1907. The game was deadlocked at four runs apiece after regulation but the Maroons pushed across two runs in the top of the tenth inning. Winnipeg hoped to add to its lead with only one away and its catcher Heinie Berger coming to the plate. Fargo pitcher Charlie Boardman, a local boy, had a history of bad blood with Berger, stemming from a near beaning earlier in the season in Winnipeg. On that occasion Berger had fired his bat out to the mound at Boardman. This time Boardman hit Berger in the shoulder with a fastball and the big catcher charged the hill, bat in hand, proceeding to hammer the pitcher repeatedly over the back with the bat. Fargo fans exploded out of the bleachers, screaming for Berger's hide, forcing the Maroon players to drag their teammate into the relative security of the dugout. Umpire Davey tried in vain to get the mob to disperse from the field so that the game could be completed. After fifteen minutes, he chose to call the game, with the score reverting to the previous inning's deadlock. Winnipeg wanted a forfeit since it was unruly Fargo fans that had prevented the contest's completion. The league ordered a replay but bad weather contrived to ultimately cancel the series and force the two teams to share the championship.

In the fallout following the base brawl Berger was ordered to pay a fine of $17.15 and apologize to Boardman. Boardman demanded and was granted $125 from Charlie Moll, a debt owed him from the previous season when he had pitched for Moll's St. Boniface Saints club. Each player on the co-champion teams received the princely sum of $38.50 as his share of the playoff receipts.

The W.C.L. reopened in 1919 with teams in Regina, Saskatoon, Moose Jaw, and Winnipeg. Alberta chose to stick with senior-league baseball but added a few interesting wrinkles like World War I flying ace "Wop" May dropping the opening-day ball from his JN 4 plane on a pass over Diamond Park. Later that season His Royal Highness, Edward, Prince of Wales, attended a game between the Calgary Hustlers and Edmonton Veterans. The prince proved to be an affable sort, mingling

"Fast Eddie and the Hustlers"
Edward, Prince of Wales, is surrounded by members of the
Calgary Hustlers baseball team in Calgary, September 1919.

with the crowd and yelling for one Calgary batter to "get a step-ladder" when he swung at a pitch that was a foot over his head.

The Winnipeg General Strike prevented the Maroons from opening their 1919 season in the newly refurbished River Park. The team played at the ragged confines of Norwood Park, but clearly any fear of a Bolshevik takeover was not affecting Winnipeg's baseball fans. When the daily papers began publishing a week later, a crowd of three thousand was cited for the professional encounter while another two thousand attended a senior-league contest at Wesley Park.

Calgary and Edmonton were back in the W.C.L. for the 1920 campaign. Politics conspired to play a part in baseball when the Edmonton Trades and Labour Council forced the Eskimos to drop a player named Bankhead who worked as a strikebreaker in the off-season. A report out of Calgary stated that four of the Broncos players were in Bankhead's employ.

The 1921 campaign began with some unseasonably cold temperatures. Snow caused the cancellation of some games, leading players from the southern climes to question their chosen profession. One contest played in Regina saw the Senators nip the Saskatoon Quakers 1-0 in eleven bone-chilling innings. The winning run crossed the plate on a play that was ruled a balk ball, but the pitcher could have just been shivering. Radio was only in its earliest stages so Regina concocted another means of alerting its fans of cancellations on game day. If the flag was flying at R. H. Williams & Sons' store, the game was on.

The W.C.L. reached its peak talent-wise that season with several of its players destined for success in the major leagues. The circuit was now Class B calibre; however, when Regina and Moose Jaw quit mid-season it sounded the death knell for the embattled league. The four remaining teams limped through the remainder of the campaign that saw Calgary defeat Winnipeg in a championship series plagued by rain in Winnipeg and snow in Calgary.

The Calgary Bronks and Edmonton Eskimos moved on to compete in the Western International League with Vancouver and Tacoma the following year. This league too was doomed to failure, disbanding in mid-June. What better way to end a section on twenty years of rugged Prairie ball than with a punch-up? The Esks and Bronks met in one final series before the season was scrapped. In this contest an umpire named

Croter struck a blow for verbally abused and physically intimidated officials everywhere. Edmonton left-fielder Red Andrews took violent exception to a called third strike and hurled his bat at the grandstand, narrowly missing putting it through the screen and injuring a patron. He was ordered off the field for his outburst, but with the league folding and no fear of a suspension, he decided not to go quietly. He charged at Croter only to be rocked by an uppercut and chased all over the diamond by the feisty official.

The predominant mind-set among the fans and the newspapers during the first two decades of the century was "go big or not at all." The clubs didn't want to admit that they were low-minor-league operations. At the slightest provocation rumours abounded that the following season would bring bigger and better baseball. This wait-until-next-year attitude impacted at the turnstiles. The result was that during the period acknowledged as the golden era of minor-league baseball, the Prairies were without a pro team.

With pro ball a memory, barnstorming units drew well throughout the twenties and thirties. The Dominion Day weekend generally brought some talented visitors to Prairie towns for games against local all-star

"Where is Everybody? I Thought We Had a Practice"
Four members of the Winnipeg Pegs, circa 1915.

contingents. Teams like Gilkerson's Colored Giants out of Chicago or the Great Northern Pacific club from St. Paul would often play four to six games in a weekend.

In Winnipeg, players in the amateur Senior League achieved near cult status during the 1920s, when the makers of Eskimo Pies included their photographs with the purchase of an ice-cream bar. Wesley Park, situated across from Wesley College (now the University of Winnipeg), was one of the first diamonds in western Canada to install lights to keep up with the demand for the facility.

"Barnstorming Babylon"
Scenic Wesley Park in Winnipeg, circa 1920. This diamond hosted
top-flight senior ball and the best touring clubs of the era.

In a move that many people thought was foolhardy, the Northern League was revived during the height of the Depression in 1933. Bruno Haas, the Maroons' new owner, knew something about adversity, having established a major-league record by giving up sixteen walks in a game while pitching for the Philadelphia Athletics. Bruno was the Bo Jackson or Deion Sanders of his era, having also played twenty-one games in the National Football League. Haas felt that in spite of the difficult financial times, Winnipeggers would part with a quarter for the opportunity to see some quality baseball. He was right!

Veteran sportswriter Vince Leah remembered Haas in a *Tribune* column written in 1954 prior to the start of the baseball season. It seems Bruno was a creature of habit, getting dressed to the waist in his baseball pants before partaking in a pregame shave in the right-field clubhouse at Sherburn Park. The tight-fisted owner seemed to have a sixth sense when it came to his precious baseballs being hit onto Portage Avenue during batting practice. At the crack of a well-hit ball, Bruno would charge from his shaving mirror half-dressed, his face covered in lather, to help his beleaguered batboys locate a baseball. This hairy apparition waving a straight razor and bellowing instructions was quite a shock to motorists heading home from work along Portage Avenue. At least one alarmed woman had to be restrained from calling the police.

The Maroons managed to capture the Northern League championship in 1935. The club ran many successful promotions, often with an eye to aiding charities. Winnipeg hosted the Northern League all-stars that season with all proceeds going toward the Associated Fresh Air Camps, offering holidays for needy children.

Unfortunately the Sherburn Park years were marred by tragedy. The Maroons' Hal Brossard was hit in the face with a relay through from second base on a potential double-play ball. The sheer velocity of the errant throw was enough to carom off Brossard's skull into the first-base bleachers where it broke the nose of Mrs. Douglas Nichols. The motionless ballplayer was carried from the field on a stretcher and rushed to hospital. A fractured skull brought an end to Brossard's promising career.

Sherburn Park did not have lights, making most games twilight contests. The evening shadows often made it difficult for a batter to pick up the ball. In late August of 1936 George Tkach, the twenty-year-old second baseman of the Superior Blues, was struck in the head by a pitch thrown by the Maroons' Alex Uffelman. Tkach was taken to the General Hospital, where early indications pointed to a full recovery; but six days later the young man succumbed to complications from his injury.

Two years later the shadows of Sherburn claimed a second victim and this time it was a much-loved Maroon player. Baseball was in the blood of Linus "Skeeter" Ebnet. He had entered the Northern League with Grand Forks at the tender age of sixteen in 1933. Three years later, he joined his cousin Ambrose with the Maroons. He was in his third year with Winnipeg, popular with his teammates and the fans, when an errant fastball claimed another victim at Sherburn Park.

The Northern League was no match for the old Western Canada League when it came to rowdy behaviour on the field or in the stands. However, on occasion the fans did vent a little spleen on what they considered to be poor officiating. The Maroons were playing the Jamestown Jimmies in the third game of the 1936 semifinals when a near riot ensued. Winnipeg trailed Jamestown by a run in the seventh inning when umpire Gharrity decided it was getting too dark to continue. The bleachers rose in unison, in what could have been a precursor to the wave, with a chant of "finish the game." A frightened Gharrity beat a hasty retreat to the clubhouse while the fans waited for several minutes, hoping that the ump would reverse his decision. Realizing that the game had been terminated, an angry mob awaited Gharrity's departure. The frightened official would only venture from his sanctuary under police escort and was whisked away in a waiting cruiser.

The following year saw another umpire-baiting debacle at Sherburn Park. Once again it was the premature ending to a contest that sparked the unpleasantness. Even Bruno Haas got into the act, blocking the path of umpire Catterlin as he tried to exit the field after calling the game for darkness. The fans surrounded the ump, screaming at him and pulling on his arm to impede his progress to the parking lot. It took a brave off-duty R.C.M.P. officer and a city police constable to escort Catterlin as far as the front gate. From there, mask in hand and cleats still on his feet, he took to his heels. A compassionate motorist took pity on the poor man and gave him a lift to his hotel. Haas was slapped with a ten-dollar fine for his part in the fracas.

Bruno Haas decided to take a more active part in his investment later that season in a game against the Wausau Lumberjacks. Winnipeg was in a jam with the bases loaded and only one out in the second inning. Haas was twenty years removed from his record base-on-balls perform-ance but felt he was the man to put out the fire. In a scene about as probable as a bad movie, he proceeded to fan the next two batters and crack a three-run homer in the bottom of the inning. The Maroons swept a double-header that day, giving the middle-aged male contingent in the crowd of two thousand a new idol.

C. H. McFayden, manager of the Osborne Stadium, bought the Maroons in 1939 and moved them into his facility. The club's new playing manager was Joe Mowry, late of the Boston Braves. Mowry found Northern League pitching to his liking, batting a torrid .367, a scant percentage point ahead of hometown hero Maroon first baseman Hugh Gustafson. An enormously successful season saw the Maroons double

"A Modicum of Joy in an Ever-Darkening World"
Winnipeg Maroons, champions of the Northern Baseball League, September 1939.

their attendance from the previous year and capture their second league championship.

As the Northern League's sole Canadian franchise – although stocked almost exclusively by American players – the Maroons were not directly affected by Canada's entry into World War II. The inevitable manpower crunch came with the bombing of Pearl Harbour. In 1942 the league began to experience difficulties brought on by the war. The Sioux Falls Canaries, en route to Winnipeg after a game in Fargo, suffered the scourge of all minor-league clubs – bus trouble. Normally this would have been resolved by renting another bus but American wartime law prohibited a second rental and the road trip had to be scrapped. This was a minor inconvenience compared to the difficulties that major-league teams on the eastern seaboard were facing. All night games were cancelled for the duration of the war for fear of an attack by German U-boats. Induction notices ultimately impacted on the playoff format that season. The Wausau Lumberjacks defeated Eau Claire in the semifinals to secure a berth in the championship. Unfortunately the club lost five players to military duty and was unable to find suitable replacements in time for the final. The league decided to make the other semifinal series between Sioux Falls and Winnipeg its championship, and the Maroons captured

"Fly-boy Fly Chasers"
An air-force ball team at No. 11 S.F.T.S. Yorkton Airbase, 1941.

a somewhat tainted championship in the circuit's final season until after the war.

North America was ready to enjoy its leisure time after the six-year horror of war, and few enterprises enjoyed greater expansion than minor-league baseball. In 1946 over thirty-two million ball fans crammed into minor-league parks – a staggering increase from the under-ten-million tickets sold the previous year. The Northern League was back and this time the clubs were affiliated with major-league organizations. Teams no longer had to beat the bushes looking for talent; the parent club provided the team with players as well as picking up their salaries. It was rumoured at the time that both the Winnipeg Maroons and Brandon Greys were planning to return to the Northern League but neither club made the move.

Manitoba was content to watch a fine calibre of senior and junior ball until 1948 when a semipro circuit came into being. It is often difficult to discern any tangible difference between some of the semiprofessional leagues and the low minors. Most semipro-club players held down jobs, preferring weekend tournament play, where a winning club had a chance at a decent payday for a couple of days' work. The semipro-league arrangements generally called for the players to get a cut of the gate receipts and not a salary paid by the club. The most notable exception to the rule were pitchers, who often hired out their services for tournaments.

The following year, the collapse of the Negro National League brought an influx of talented black ballplayers to Manitoba. Fans who had marvelled at the talents of many of these players when they passed through town while barnstorming with clubs like the Birmingham Black Barons or Chicago American Giants now had the opportunity to watch them on a regular basis. The 1949 final series pitted the Brandon Greys against the Elmwood Giants. The series went to a seventh and deciding game that was played at Brandon's Kinsmen Memorial Park before a record crowd of fifty-two hundred fans. The clash was so widely anticipated that fans drove in from Saskatchewan and North Dakota to witness it. They were treated to a classic pitchers' duel that saw the clubs deadlocked at a run apiece in the fifteenth inning. Finally Brandon starter Frank Watkins took matters into his own hands, lashing a single to left field that scored the speedy Rafe Cabrera with the winning run. Watkins tossed all fifteen innings, being matched pitch for pitch by the Giants' Hal Price. The calibre of fielding in the game was remarkable; Cabrera ranged all over the diamond while handling his seventeen chances at second base. The jubilant Greys hoisted their weary hurler on their shoulders and paraded him around the ballpark to screams of approval from their adoring fans.

"Night Ball Comes to Renfrew Park"
The first night game played at Edmonton's Renfrew Park between
the Edmonton Eskimos and Calgary Braves in 1947.

In 1950 the Minot Mallards entered the circuit, giving birth to the Man Dak League. During its five-year existence this league, stocked mainly with black players too old to be considered prospects for the majors, provided Manitoba with some of the finest baseball ever witnessed.

After a twenty-five-year hiatus from the pro game, Alberta launched the semiprofessional Big Four Inter-City League that lasted from 1947 to 1952. The Calgary Stampeders and Edmonton Eskimos – names far more familiar from football – competed in the Class A Western International League in 1953–54. Edmonton topped the league in attendance its first year but the minor leagues were in a period of decline and the league folded. It was too early for television to be siphoning off fans from the minor-league affiliates; the true culprit was radio, as the unrestricted broadcasting of major-league games undermined attendance down at the local ball field.

"Quintessential Prairie Ball"
Sports Day, May 24, 1949, at Wilcox, Saskatchewan.

By 1950 Saskatchewan had its own semipro circuit, the Southern League. The province also hosted some of the country's most hotly contested cash tournaments. A $5200 affair at Swift Current that year was so well attended that bleachers had to be moved from the Frontier Day grounds to Mitchell Field to satisfy the demand for seating.

In 1951 Medicine Hat joined the circuit and the Western Canada League was revised. "Red" Nixon was a flamboyant promoter who owned the Swift Current club of the W.C.L. as well as a purely touring nine from Sceptre. He chose Edmonton's Renfrew Park as the site for the richest cash tournament ever contested on the Prairies. The event called for $7200 in prize money with a cool $2500 as the winners' share. Many of the W.C.L. players were American college ballplayers who could not resist the lure of the cash tournaments, and many clubs reported players AWOL when league play resumed on the Monday after the tournament. Rain contrived to wash out the finale between the California Mohawks and Eston Ramblers, but at least one Edmontonian went home happy. Annis Stukus, coach of the Edmonton Eskimos football club, got a tip from Don Fleming of the *Edmonton Journal* that the talented college football player Rollie Miles was in town for the tournament with the Regina Caps. Stukus hustled down to the ballpark to offer Miles a tryout with the Eskimos; Rollie returned to Edmonton after the baseball season to star in the C.F.L. for twelve years.

The perils of hiring students during a rainy summer came back to haunt the league finalists in 1951. Indian Head and Moose Jaw were unable to field teams due to widespread defections back to American campuses.

In 1953 when the W.C.L. dropped to only four franchises, the circuit played an interlocking schedule with the Man Dak League. The wily veterans from the Negro Leagues proved too good for the college boys who made up the bulk of the W.C.L. rosters.

The new W.C.L. and its offshoot the Can-Am League were often plagued with financial woes during their fourteen-year existence; however, the circuit produced some exciting baseball and one of the oddest game delays on record. It was mid-August 1961 and the Medicine Hat Meridians were hosting the Lethbridge White Sox. The game was in the sixth inning when a horde of moths descended onto the diamond. Visibility became so bad that White Sox third baseman Danny Salazar took a pitch in the head that he never saw. Umpire Bob Porter could barely make out the outfielders, and the infield grass looked like the aftermath of a blizzard. At the height of the infestation the game was called and the park lights turned off. Five minutes later when the power was restored, there wasn't a moth in sight, and Medicine Hat went on to a 7-5 victory.

In 1954, Mark Danzker brought professional baseball back to Winnipeg when he purchased the Sioux Falls Canaries' franchise, securing the Class C Northern League affiliate of the St. Louis Cardinals. The Winnipeg Goldeyes played out of a new $100,000 ballpark at the south end of the football stadium. This meant the end of Winnipeg's franchise in the Man Dak League but the Brandon Greys often rented Osborne Stadium, drawing large crowds of fans still dedicated to the semipro circuit.

This was my first glimpse at pro ball. Two bits got you a seat in the first- or third-base bleachers. If you were lucky enough to grab a foul ball you got a free pass to the next game. The hometown Goldeyes were always in white while the opposition wore dingy grey uniforms that looked like they had never seen the inside of a washing machine. I'd never seen a black or Latin American prior to my initial trips to the ballpark in 1957. I still remember the Goldeyes' third baseman Julio Gotay as being my first local hero.

As a kid I got to watch future Hall of Famers like Willie Stargell of the Grand Forks Chiefs, Lou Brock and Gaylord Perry of the St. Cloud Rox, and Jim Palmer of the Aberdeen Pheasants. A couple of players

"Don't Muss My Hair"
Winnipeg Goldeyes left to right: Roger Robinson, Ray Oliver, Lou Brown,
Roberto Herrera and Chico Sarez congratulate Bill Carpenter on a
pennant-clinching 7-2 win over Aberdeen in September 1959.

who deserve more recognition for their skills on the diamond but unfortunately are better known for their legal troubles got started in the Northern League. Denny McLain pitched for the Duluth Superior Dukes while Orlando Cepeda won the Northern League equivalent of the triple crown with St. Cloud in 1956.

Unlike any of the previous teams to play on the Prairies, the Goldeyes' salaries were being paid by St. Louis; this major-league affiliation offered the circuit financial stability and an air of longevity. Most players came to Winnipeg at the behest of the parent club to hone their skills before trying to claw their way up the minor-league ladder. Incidents of umpire baiting and brawling were extremely rare. Winnipeg consistently outdrew its American rivals, treating the fans to league championships in 1957, 1959, and 1960. The Goldeyes even had their games televised on occasion but the network executives showed where their priorities lay when they pre-empted a tight contest with Duluth in the ninth inning so that the *Wild Bill Hickock* show could be seen in its entirety.

"The Rifleman Loads Up"
Chuck Connors, TV's "Rifleman," prepares to hit during a 1960
promotion; Goldeyes manager Walter Kurowski is the catcher.

In 1962 the road-weary St. Louis Cardinals eschewed a rare day off from their National League schedule to come to Winnipeg and lay a whipping on the Goldeyes. Local *Tribune* reporter John Robertson marvelled at the patience of Stan "the Man" Musial as he handled hackneyed questions from the local scribes with class and dignity.

Winnipeg was never in contention in 1964 but its Puerto Rican slugger Felix Deleon had designs on capturing the home-run and RBI titles. Going into the final game of the season Deleon trailed Andy Kosco of the Bismarck Mandan Pards by a single homer and a lone run batted in. Felix smashed a round-tripper during the finale but in his excitement did not look where he was running. Puerto Rican countryman and close friend Victor Torres was on first base and made the mistake of stopping to admire the flight of the ball, allowing Deleon to pass him on the base path. Felix was called out on the play, enabling Kosco to capture the triple crown. It was a long trip back to Puerto Rico for Torres, and his pal Felix refused to speak to him.

After the 1964 campaign the Goldeyes took the rather extreme position of exercising a silent protest over the firing of Cardinal general manager Bing Devine and the resignation of skipper Johnny Keane, and terminated their affiliation with St. Louis. The move left the Northern League without one of its pivotal franchises for five years until Winnipeg returned in 1969 as the Class A farm club of the expansion Kansas City Royals. The Northern League had reverted to a shortened season of only seventy games. While all of its opponents had farm systems already in place, Winnipeg had to wait for players to trickle down to it through the newly arranged Royal system. The Goldeyes struggled to a miserable last-place finish, doing very poorly at the gate. In a scene reminiscent of earlier times, a late shipment of baseballs almost saw the club start its final home stand without enough game balls. Despite the year of growing pains, Randy Moffat was prepared to keep the team in the city until fate intervened.

Winnipeg lawyer and businessman Maitland Steinkopf was in Montreal visiting his cousin Charles Bronfman, the owner of the Montreal Expos. Half jokingly, Steinkopf asked Bronfman when he was planning to send a Triple A franchise to Winnipeg. Both men had a good chuckle as the Expos' top farm club was firmly entrenched in Buffalo, a city with a ninety-four-year history of professional baseball. That very week Bronfman heard from Expos president John McHale that the Buffalo Bisons were on the brink of financial ruin. Steinkopf prolonged his vacation, making several calls to Winnipeg, and by mid-June a city in the heart of the Canadian Prairies was playing in the predominantly American East Coast International League. In hindsight the move was doomed to failure; Winnipeg, because of its remote locale, was forced to pick up seventy-five percent of the visiting teams' travel costs. The Winnipeg Whips in their eighteen-month existence were a disaster on the playing field as well as at the gate. That isn't to say that local fans didn't get to watch the likes of Bobby Grich, Don Baylor, and Carlton Fisk; the trouble was they all played for the opposing teams. Montreal pulled the plug on the Whips after the 1971 season. The club moved to Peninsula, Virginia, where it drew half as many fans while still managing to finish last.

"Safe at Third"
Jim Gosger slides into third base in a cloud of dust during the
Winnipeg Whips' contest against the Richmond Braves in July 1971.

Pro baseball reappeared on the Prairies in 1975 in Lethbridge, Alberta, when the Montreal Expos moved their rookie affiliate into the Pioneer League. This was a short-season summer league that generally attracted crowds in the neighbourhood of a thousand people. Fans got a chance to see young prospects at the earliest stage of their professional development. The degree of difficulty in attaining the pinnacle of the profession can be illustrated by contrasting the careers of two young Lethbridge sluggers. In the team's inaugural season Andre Dawson led the league with thirteen home runs. The "Hawk," despite playing through myriad knee injuries, has gone on to post Hall of Fame numbers in the big leagues over the past twenty years. Two years later when Lethbridge was the Los Angeles Dodgers' rookie affiliate, Mike Zouras slammed twenty-one home runs, a record that still stands for the Pioneer League. He never played a game in the "bigs."

Lethbridge departed the circuit after the 1983 season to return ten years later as an independent franchise. The Lethbridge Mounties were stocked by players from a number of organizations.

Two other Pioneer League franchises have operated in Alberta. Medicine Hat has been home to the Toronto Blue Jays' rookies since 1977. Calgary operated a team in the loop from 1977 to 1984. Initially aligned with the St. Louis Cardinals, the club switched allegiance to the Montreal Expos in 1979. Calgary fans got to watch the young Andres Galaragga, while Medicine Hat fans saw Lloyd Moseby when he was a Toronto first-round draft choice.

Peter Pocklington, owner of the Edmonton Oilers and the man who signed Canadian icon Wayne Gretzky's pay cheque, purchased the Ogden A's franchise of the Pacific Coast League and brought Triple A baseball to Edmonton in 1981. The Trappers were initially aligned with the Chicago White Sox but captured their lone league championship under the banner of the California Angels in 1984. That season a fair Edmonton club managed to capture the first half of the season with a record only two games above the .500 mark. The team played to a losing record in the second half but stumbled into some marvellous good fortune in the playoffs. Its opponents the Salt Lake City Gulls were pure poison at the box office that season, only finishing the campaign through league intervention. At one point the team's electricity was turned off, telephone services cut, and radio broadcasts cancelled. The league ensured that the stadium lights were turned on to complete the season but insisted that the Gulls play all their playoff games in Edmonton. The friendly confines of the newly renamed John Ducey Park helped the Trappers secure a trip to the finals. Again scheduling played into Edmonton's hands. The Southern Division-champion Hawaii Islanders were prevented from playing any home games due to a booking conflict at their stadium. Rain washed out the first two contests in Edmonton, and rather than attempt a reschedule, the series

Back Row (l-r) — Reggie West, Craig Gerber, Al Romero, Tim Krauss, Chris Clark. Middle Row (l-r) — Mike Browning, Kirk McCaskill, Stu Cliburn, Rick Adams, Steve Finch, Jay Kibbe, Pat Keedy, Steve Liddle, Rick Steirer, Steve Brown, Joe Simpson, James Randall, Darrin Stapleton (Clubhouse Boy). Front Row (l-r) — Dave Smith, Marty Kain, Darrell Miller, Frank Reberger (Coach), Moose Stubing (Manager), Ed Ott (Coach), Bill Mooneyham, Steve Lubratich, Leonard Garcia (Trainer). Bat Boys — Norm Rust, Graham Kenny. Photo by Action Photography.

"The Best Triple A Has to Offer"
The Pacific Coast League champions for 1984, the Edmonton Trappers.

was now a best-of-three affair. Good luck can only carry a team so far; if the Trappers hoped to win the championship it meant beating two of the league's best pitchers. Mike Bielecki posted a gaudy 19-3 record during the regular season for the Islanders but the Trappers managed to take the opener 8-4. The second game would be no easier as Hawaii countered with its eighteen-game winner Alonso Pulido. It made no difference to the "team of destiny" as Edmonton rode homers from Pat Keedy and Tim Krauss to a 9-6 triumph and the league championship. Adding to the string of unprecedented good fortune, Canadian-born Kirk McCaskill got the victory.

The Calgary Cannons replaced the Salt Lake City Gulls in the Pacific Coast League in 1985. Russ and Diane Parker had been part of the ownership consortium for Calgary's Pioneer League franchise but undertook the Triple A operation by themselves. The couple applied some of the business initiative from their successful Canon copier franchise to the marketing of baseball. A deal was struck with Molson Breweries for the club's broadcasting rights, and local businesses could purchase advertising space on the outfield fence for four thousand dollars. The team saw some very talented players pass through the organization in its first ten years. Unfortunately, as the farm club of a perennial also-ran like the Seattle Mariners, there was no guarantee how long prospects would remain in the Cannons' roster. The team managed to make it to the postseason in 1985, 1987, and 1991. The first year, the Mariners called up Pacific Coast League MVP Danny Tartabull prior to the playoffs. In 1991 Calgary made it out of the Northern Division and into the league championship only to have its proposed starter Dave Fleming called up to Seattle on the eve of pitching the most important game in franchise history. The Cannons went down to defeat, leaving the Parkers to seriously question their working arrangement with the Mariners.

The return of the Lethbridge Mounties to the Pioneer League in 1992 meant that the four Alberta cities that started the Western Canada League in 1907 were the lone proponents of the pro game on the Prairies. Sam Katz had managed to bring a couple of Triple A games featuring Calgary and Edmonton to Winnipeg, but Manitoba had been without a pro club for twenty-three years. Saskatchewan still ran some first-class cash tournaments but its last semi-pro team, the Saskatoon Blues, had folded after

A Cannon blasts around the base path.

the 1964 campaign. The Toronto Blue Jays' back-to-back World Series triumphs in 1992–93 were just the catalyst that the Prairies needed to revive interest in professional baseball.

BARNSTORMING

IT WOULD BE IMPOSSIBLE TO TRACE THE FIRST CLUB EVER TO BARNSTORM ON the Canadian Prairies. As mentioned earlier, Walter Scott pitched for a squad that toured Saskatchewan by train in the 1880s, and the various Bloomer troupes were making trips northward by the turn of the century. In 1874 one of the most ambitious tours took place when Henry Chadwick and Al Spalding took eighteen ballplayers to Great Britain to compete against some of the local cricketers.

Barnstorming to me conjures up visions of touring black teams traversing the countryside in dilapidated jalopies. The Cuban Giants, a group of waiters from the Argyle Hotel in Trenton, New Jersey, were the first black club to go out on the road. The team had played in the Eastern Interstate League until being banished on racial grounds. Although none of the players was from Cuba, the club adopted the name in the hope of deflecting racial intolerance. These Giants toured the eastern United States, taking on any amateur or pro nine that would give them a game.

Teams would often resort to gimmickry to attract crowds. The Page Fence Giants of Michigan often arrived in a town early, riding bicycles through the streets and carrying placards to advertise a game or drum up competition. Another early barnstorming unit, the All-American Black Tourists, arrived at the ballpark in full dress suits, accessorized with opera hats and silk umbrellas. The carnival atmosphere that surrounded these teams did little to mask the talent of some of the country's finest ballplayers.

While not privy to the original wave of talented touring black teams, the Prairies did play host to some of the finest barnstorming squads of the early decades of this century. Baseball owes a great debt to J. L. Wilkinson, a white promoter from Kansas City, Missouri. He was the first owner of the great Kansas City Monarchs of the Negro League and the originator of night baseball. In 1929, the Monarchs began travelling with floodlights and a generator, a move that enabled the touring club to squeeze in three and often four games a day. The extra revenue amassed from these night encounters was vital to the club's financial survival. The lights cast a pale glow over the field and dimmed dramatically with every sputter of the generator. A length of cloth covered the fences to allow the batter a better glimpse at the white blur that was rocketing toward him. The lights were mounted on fifty-foot poles standing on a flatbed truck, leaving the fielders without a clue on any high pop fly that carried above the system.

One of Wilkinson's first and most popular creations was a team called All Nations founded in 1914. True to its name, the club featured blacks, whites, Indians, Asians, Latin Americans, and often women. The team's starting pitching was the envy of any major-league roster, with the two great black hurlers, John Donaldson and Bill Drake, and fireballing Cuban Jose Mendez. Along with outfielder Cristobel Torriente, this trio went on to form the nucleus of the Monarchs when the Negro League was formed in 1920.

Another perennial fan favourite was the House of David. In 1903, Benjamin Purnell, an Ohio farmer, felt that he had experienced a revelation while he slept. In his dream a white dove had perched on his shoulder, proclaimed him the Sixth Son of the House of David, and empowered him to unite the Lost Tribes of Israel before the Judgment Day. Purnell attracted a group of followers whom he convinced to renounce their worldly possessions and establish the House of David Colony in Benton Harbour, Michigan. Purnell was polygamous, alleged to have taken several wealthy widows as brides while his colonists were forced to adhere to his strict rules – no sex, no smoking, no drinking, and no shaving.

This final religious tenet made the males of the colony somewhat of a novelty. Curiosity seekers drove from as far away as Chicago to get a glimpse of the bearded colonists. Seeking an opportunity to turn a profit, Purnell built an amusement park. In 1910 the colony started staging ball games, and the squad was soon proficient enough to capture three consecutive titles in the semipro Benton Harbour Industrial League. The club drew large crowds during a tour of the Midwest, catching the eye of a New York promoter. The Davids took the East Coast by storm and soon were touring all over the continent. Purnell's wife, dubbed Queen Mary by the press, often travelled with the team and acted as manager.

Like many early sixties rock groups, the House of David spawned a host of cheap imitations. There was, for example, the Black House of David out of Havana, Cuba, whose members eschewed a razor for the season but had nothing to do with the sect. The original House of David was good enough to draw thirty thousand fans out to Shibe Park in Philadelphia in 1926. Its shortstop, Dutch Faust, had the talent to be offered a contract by Connie Mack (real name Cornelius McGilicuddy), owner of the Philadelphia Athletics, but he remained true to his religion. Winnipeg's own "Snake" Siddle, a long-time star of the local senior leagues, toured with the Davids. Later when the club had a hard time filling out a roster from within its ranks, honorary Davids like Babe Ruth

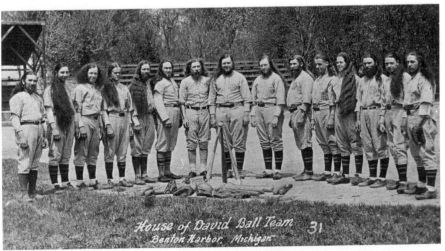

"The Bewhiskered Belters"
The 1931 House of David touring ball team.

and Grover Cleveland Alexander donned false beards and took to the field. These two gentlemen would have had particular difficulty with the no-alcohol principle of the religion.

Despite the fact that the club toured for over forty years, very little has been written about the Davids. The *Regina Leader Post* ran an interesting article about the team on July 4, 1950. Manager George Anderson, the lone member of the sect still playing on the team, had joined the squad in 1928. He felt that the 1933 roster was the best team in the history of the franchise. That club had defeated the St. Louis Cardinals 8-4 in a contest played during the regular season. This was no third-rate Cardinal club but the venerable "Gashouse Gang," featuring the Dean brothers, Leo Durocher, Ducky Medwick, and Pepper Martin – the team that won the World Series the following year. With a starting rotation augmented by retired major leaguers Albert "Chief" Bender and Grover Cleveland Alexander, the '33 Davids went on to play 175 games that year, losing only twelve.

Anderson vividly recalled the origin of the team's trademark pepper game. It started with Doc Tally, Dutch Faust and Zeke Bouske clowning around before a game, testing each other's reflexes. Those in attendance were mesmerized by their sleight of hand, and it became a part of the team's routine. In 1935 the constant life on the road almost caught up with some of the team members. Having finished a date in Fargo, the Davids were driving to Winnipeg when one of their cars crashed. The vehicle flipped three times but miraculously no one was badly hurt. In the tradition of all great performers, the show had to go on: stiff and sore, the players took to the field that evening in Winnipeg and had the crowd chortling with antics such as wiping the plate off with their beards when the umpire made a bad call.

Another white club that was only too happy to compete against Negro League teams was the Brooklyn Bushwicks. The Bushwicks were the most successful independent ball club in America. Their home field, Dexter Park in Queens, was the first facility to install permanent lights. The Brooklyners played against the top black teams in weekend double-headers, often hiring young phenomenons on their way up to the majors or old pros on the way down. Dizzy Dean suited up with the club on several occasions. During a hectic schedule in 1936 the club hired Waite Hoyt, the recently retired Yankee and future Hall of Famer, to pitch for it. Hoyt faced the Pittsburgh Crawfords in his debut before a standing-room-only crowd of seventeen thousand. He pitched brilliantly, giving up only two hits, but was beaten 2-0 on Pittsburgh's Theoli "Fireball" Smith's one-hitter.

By the 1930s black baseball had several teams that could rival basketball's Harlem Globetrotters in their ability to mix humour with great athleticism. A New York promoter, Syd Pollock, was the front man for the Zulu Cannibal Baseball Tribe. The club played in African tribal paint and hula skirts and, although popular with white audiences, was scorned by black organizations for reinforcing a negative stereotype.

Another of these novelty-act teams was Miami's Ethiopian Clowns, a frequent visitor to the Prairies. The team later moved to Cincinnati under the tutelage of Harlem Globetrotter owner Abe Saperstein. The club had a routine known as "shadow ball," where they pantomimed an infield practice. Its act included a dwarf named Spec Bebop and a player dressed up as King Tut. On the field the team relied on the natural comic skills of pitcher Peanuts Nyasses (a.k.a. Johnny Davis) and first baseman "Goose" Tatum, who later toured with the Globetrotters. Catcher Pepper Basset often played his position from a rocking chair but still gunned out any runner who dared to try and steal a base.

With too much talent to remain strictly barnstormers, the Clowns joined the Negro League in 1942. The club moved to Indianapolis and, in 1953, as the Negro League was winding down, signed a woman, Toni Stone, as its second baseman. Stone justified the club's confidence by batting .267. The Clowns were the longest-standing barnstorming club in North America, still touring Canadian ballparks well into the 1960s. When the club played in Winnipeg in 1964 its new gimmick was a midget shortstop. The diminutive Billie Vaughan stood only four foot five inches tall but dazzled in the field with his lightning reflexes and bullet throws to first base.

Canada had its own touring black clubs during the 1920s. Charlie Ross's Black Sox and the Winnipeg Giants both successfully barnstormed in Alberta. Dominion Day was popular for touring teams; they would often play as many as five games against local squads. Arthur Conan Doyle attended a match between a Minneapolis club and the Winnipeg all-stars on July 1, 1923. Despite admitting to being an old cricketer, Doyle felt that the fielding and hitting witnessed that afternoon far outstripped his native game.

"Elementary, My Dear Watson"
Sir Arthur Conan Doyle takes a ripple during a visit to
Jasper National Park in June 1914.

Power has long been a dimension of the game that the public clamours to see, and the barnstormers often carried several hitters capable of producing tape-measure shots. Gilkerson's Colored Giants drew four thousand fans out to a double-header at Winnipeg's Wesley Park in 1927. This initial two-game series was so popular that the visitors were asked to remain in town another day for a second double-header. It was during the prolonged engagement that the Giants' catcher Joseph hit a ball that rocketed over the left-field fence, clearing the bleachers before it ultimately came to rest at the steps of United College.

Promoters were not averse to using well-known celebrities to boost gate receipts. A crowd of thirty-five hundred fans turned out to Mewata Park in Calgary to see a guest appearance by silent-movie western star "Hoot" Gibson. In town to scout a movie location, Gibson was to appear at the ballpark to bat against Calgary's mayor in a promotional stunt. Unfortunately, he didn't appear. Calgarians had better luck fifty years later when Jim Bouton, the infamous author of the book *Ball Four*, pitched a game for the Calgary Jimmies of the Alberta Senior League. Well past his glory years with the New York Yankees, Bouton still managed to handcuff the Barrhead Cardinals 7-0.

Promoter Lee Dillage's team out of Minot, North Dakota, toured Saskatchewan in the luxury of a Dusenburg car in the mid-1920s. The squad sported two "ringers" in Swede Risberg and Hap Flesch, late of the Chicago Black Sox scandal infamy. The two were barred from playing organized baseball but eked out a living playing in cash tournaments and semipro leagues. The legendary "Shoeless" Joe Jackson had serious misgivings about "throwing" the series but feared reprisal from Risberg if he contacted the authorities. At the height of their celebrity, Risberg and Flesch rode in the back seat of the Dusenburg as it led a motor cavalcade to a town's local diamond. When the novelty of seeing the two banished players wore off, they were shunted into one of the trailing cars and replaced by some of Minot's loveliest prostitutes. The hookers stopped off at the local hotel and became a sidelight to the ball game.

One of Canada's best barnstorming teams was the Toronto Oslers who boasted hockey great Lionel Conacher, voted Canada's Athlete of the Half-Century in 1950, on their squad. The Oslers were particularly strong in the late 1920s; their catcher Hoose belted four towering home runs in a 19-5 drubbing of a Calgary all-star team. After viewing the Oslers, Calgarians felt the team was far superior to both the House of David and the Texas Colored Giants, who had passed through earlier in the summer.

The history of barnstorming is filled with interesting anecdotes like the time that a huge crowd turned out at Wesley Park to see a Victoria Day clash between Gilkerson's Colored Giants and a semipro club from Bismarck, North Dakota. It was 1934 and Satchel Paige, feeling unappreciated by the Pittsburgh Crawfords of the Negro League, had jumped ship, selling his services to auto-dealer Neil Campbell's Bismarck nine. The ball fans of Winnipeg saw a fine contest that evening but not Paige. "Ol Satch," as he called himself, was a terror on the highways and spent the weekend in an American jail.

In the autumn of 1932 western Canada was in for a special treat. The Toronto Maple Leafs and the Montreal Royals toured the Prairies at the end of the International League season. That October, news was even more exciting when Earl Mack, son of the legendary Connie, brought a touring squad of major-league all-stars. The gilt-edged squad included Heinie Manush and "Babe" Herman (both familiar to fans of the W.C.L.)

and hard-throwing Lefty Grove. However, the most widely anticipated performers were pitcher Lefty Gomez and catcher Bill Dickey, the battery for the New York Yankees in the World Series-clinching game. Dickey may have needed the extra cash after being fined a thousand dollars for breaking the jaw of Washington outfielder Carl Reynolds in a fracas. Cutting short his honeymoon, Dickey drove all the way from New York, catching up with the tour in Regina.

"A Visit from the Show"
Earl Mack's American League all-stars at
Edmonton's Renfrew Park in October 1934.

Mack clearly neglected to consult the *Farmers' Almanac* before booking a tour in western Canada in October. The squad had planned to play three games in Winnipeg. The first contest was held on a freezing-cold Friday night at the newly lighted Wesley Park. The local all-stars could only muster two hits in dropping a 6-0 decision. The next afternoon was even colder with only a thousand brave souls turning out to see a 12-8 victory for the big leaguers. Lefty Grove pitched with a thin glove over his throwing hand and was still unhittable. The night contest had to be cancelled due to the cold. Grove duplicated the dual-glove routine in Virden. The tour saw better weather in Saskatchewan but one of its Alberta dates had to be cancelled due to a windstorm.

Two years later another major-league contingent stopped off in Winnipeg. The marquee attraction on this tour was Jimmie Foxx, the

Philadelphia Athletic slugger, who was rapidly supplanting Babe Ruth as the game's premier power-hitter. A sparse crowd of a thousand turned out to watch the big leaguers play a team from North Dakota. The game very nearly ended in tragedy when Foxx was hit in the head by an errant fastball. The popular player spent a week at Winnipeg's General Hospital while Connie Mack badgered the local press with long-distance calls for news of his star. "Double X" was holding an ice-pack to his head when Ralph Allan interviewed him for the *Winnipeg Tribune*. The slugger's sole concern was "the hell he would have to pay" when his wife found out about the accident.

The following year, Japan's best club, the Dai Nippon Tokyo Giants, came to Winnipeg for a series of exhibition games against local amateur all-star contingents. The *Winnipeg Tribune* praised the Japanese squad for its power hitting as the visitors slammed four round-trippers en route to sweeping a double-header by scores of 15-0 and 4-3. Victor Starffin, the Russo-Japanese hurler, limited the locals to four hits in the series opener.

A final tour featuring former major-league stars passed through Winnipeg in 1945. The Honus Wagner All-Stars boasted the only brother act to be inducted into the Baseball Hall of Fame: Paul and Lloyd Waner. This time the team travelled with its own opposition in the Pittsburgh Crawfords. This incarnation of the Crawfords was not the perennial contender of the old Negro National League but a squad in the fledgling United States League. The creation of Branch Rickey, a strong advocate for the desegregation of baseball, the new league was comprised mainly of younger black players who were being groomed to break the colour barrier. Winnipeg fans were treated to four well-played games between two evenly matched clubs.

The war not only took its toll on the major leagues but dipped into the talent pool available for barnstorming. Tony Allan, covering a contest for the *Winnipeg Tribune* in 1943 between the Cincinnati Clowns and the Birmingham Black Barons, was appalled by the sloppy fielding of the two black squads. He described the display as "portly gents who seemed to experience trouble getting about on their creaking underpinnings."

Allan was an ardent admirer of black baseball, despite his criticism of the current state of the game with many of the top young players fighting overseas. "What we like most about the Negro clubs' brand of baseball is their flair for doing the unexpected. They never follow a set routine and if the situation calls for a certain play, you can almost be sure they will choose an unorthodox alternative."

Allan liked the risk taking that was such a big part of the black game. A batter making a hit with two out was seldom satisfied to play it safe by stopping at first, and always tried to take the extra base to get into scoring position. The hitter always put the onus on the fielder to retrieve the ball quickly and make a perfect throw back to the infield.

Another interesting sidelight to a ball game occurred on July 12, 1945, at Winnipeg's Osborne Stadium. It had been nine years since the great Jesse Owens spat in the face of Hitler's theories about Aryan superiority by capturing four gold medals at the Berlin Olympics. Now Owens had been reduced to running races of another kind. He twice defeated the local racehorse Early Buck in a prelude to a contest between the Philadelphia Hilldales and the Detroit Giants. He then competed in base-running contests against the fastest men from both clubs. Owens' was not the only dazzling performance that evening as the Hilldales' Jim Arthur tossed a no-hitter in a 19-0 romp.

Barnstorming wound down dramatically after Jackie Robinson broke the colour barrier in 1947. Now black ballplayers had the opportunity to compete in "the show" and not be relegated to putting on a show. However, two of black baseball's greatest stars continued to barnstorm the Prairies. In 1950 James "Cool Papa" Bell was made the playing manager of the Kansas City Stars, the minor-league affiliate of the Kansas City Monarchs. The team was called the Stars or Travellers when playing in the Monarchs' territory but outside the midwestern states went by the Monarchs' moniker, no doubt to attract bigger crowds. Bell played in Saskatchewan with players like Elston Howard and Ernie Banks under his tutelage.

"Cool Papa" used to say he was so fast that he could turn out the lights and be under the covers before the room got dark. His pal Satchel Paige's retort was that Bell always liked his bed close to the door. Paige was the king of the barnstormers, playing all over North America, Mexico, and Latin America in a career that spanned five decades. He even has a Canadian connection. In the early 1960s Paige used to summer in Spy Hill, Saskatchewan, and, despite being in his late fifties, had a touring club. He recalled that the only problem with the squad was that no one would come out to see it play if he didn't pitch.

Saskatchewan is interesting from a barnstorming perspective because it attracted some of the more obscure touring clubs. The summer of 1948 saw a female nine, the Harlem Queens, defeat the local Regina Seals before seventeen hundred spectators at Taylor Field. That same summer a male club called the Brooklyn Cuban Giants played the Southern League all-stars to a 2-2 tie in front of three thousand fans at Taylor Field. Later the New Orleans Creoles, who boasted Marcenia Toni Stone at second base before she graduated to the Indianapolis Clowns of the Negro League, played in Regina.

One touring club, the San Francisco Sea Lions, disbanded while on a tour of Saskatchewan, with many of its players staying on to compete in the Southern League.

For those of us growing up in the sixties, the only real barnstorming that we got to see was the great fastball showman Eddie Feigner. Feigner toured as the King and His Court with a squad that included only three other players. A pitcher of Feigner's ability didn't need any defence; he struck hitters out while blindfolded, pitched from second base, or threw behind his back.

Another, lesser-known touring fastball troupe, the Queen and Her Maids, drew two thousand fans out to a contest at Winnipeg's Charlie Krupp Memorial Stadium in 1968. This squad was the brainchild of Royal Beaird, the father of teen pitching sensation Roundhouse Rosie. The self-proclaimed queen was good enough to play semiprofessional fastball in Los Angeles at the age of twelve. By the age of sixteen, she had racked up close to five thousand strikeouts, fifty-four shutouts, forty-eight no-hitters, and ten perfect games. The maids included two of Rosie's younger sisters and a younger brother in a wig and lipstick. The barnstormers defeated the Greater Winnipeg Senior Girls' all-stars with Rosie pitching from second base, on her knees, or with her fielders on the bench.

I had the pleasure of seeing a barnstorming contest in the summer of 1994 when the Colorado Springs Silver Bullets made a stopover in Winnipeg. The team had planned to play the Northern League all-stars but an earlier exhibition game proved to be a mismatch. The Bullets were the first women's team to attempt to compete against men. Their

"Time for a Change"
Future Hall of Famer Phil
Niekro visits the mound for
a pitching change at
Winnipeg Stadium in May
1994 during a contest
between the Silver Bullets
and Native Sons.

opponents that evening turned out to be the St. Boniface Native Sons, a fine Intermediate League team.

The Bullets, ably coached by Phil and Joe Niekro, were slick fielders but did not hit in a 10-0 loss. Still it was a thrill to see the first women's professional baseball team to operate since the All American Girls' League folded in 1954.

"Don't Even Think about It, Pal"
The Colorado Springs Silver Bullets' first baseman holds a
St. Boniface Native Son on base during their May 1994 encounter in Winnipeg.

The Silver Bullets were 6-37 in their opening year of operation. The team began facing stiff competition and ultimately settled in to playing against amateur clubs with players over the age of thirty. During their second year out on the road the Bullets improved dramatically, posting an 11-33 record against mostly semipro-level squads. The women were in most contests, dropping fourteen of their games by two runs and another eight by a single run. Manager Phil Niekro felt his club was improving with every game. The club batting average rose from .141 to .183 while its ERA plummeted two full points to 5.08. The Bullets nearly doubled their run production and were only shut out three times during the course of the year. It is the kind of grit and dedication shown by this fine touring club that will go a long way to overcome the cynicism that so many diehard fans are feeling toward the game.

SIX DIAMOND CLASSICS

IN REVIEWING SOME OF THE HIGHLIGHTS OF THE FIRST NINETY YEARS OF professional baseball on the Prairies, one could get the impression that the game revolved around brawling on the diamond and hooliganism in the stands. To the contrary, there have been some epic clashes contested. The six that I have chosen to cover provide a cross-section of the various leagues that competed during this century.

In 1919 the Winnipeg Maroons knew they faced an uphill battle when squaring off against the heavily favoured Saskatoon Quakers for the Western Canada League championship. Winnipeg had clinched a trip to the postseason by setting the league's best record in the first half of the season. However, by the end of the campaign, second-half winner Saskatoon could boast fifteen more victories. To make matters worse, the Maroons lost the services of their sure-handed shortstop Mickey Jordan to an appendicitis attack after the first game of the series. Jack Sheehan, the club's player-manager, was forced to fill in at short. The series was deadlocked at two games apiece on August 30 when the teams took the field before a crowd of three thousand fans at Winnipeg's River Park. Little Leo Seiffert, a converted outfielder, drew the starting assignment for Winnipeg while Saskatoon countered with its ace Lester King Stevenson.

Nerves played a part early in the contest. Seiffert bobbled a routine chopper back to the mound, allowing the game's first hitter, Bernie Neis, to reach base. It looked grim for the home side when Joe Kernan drilled a double on a hit-and-run play. Seiffert intentionally walked the dangerous "Chief" Williams to load the sacks with only one away. But the Maroon defence tightened, nailing Neis on a forced play at the plate, then retiring Byers on a hot smash to Sheehan for the final put-out at second. The first inning would be the only difficulty Seiffert had during the first nine innings of the game. Unfortunately for the Maroons, Stevenson was also at the peak of his game that afternoon. Neither hurler had given up a run after regulation.

Both starters remained in the contest; the concept of relief pitching was foreign to teams carrying such sparse rosters. Saskatoon threatened in the top of the twelfth, getting a runner to third base with only one out. Seiffert walked his counterpart Stevenson to load the bases with two down. Neis followed with a scorcher to Sheehan that the classy veteran scooped cleanly, stepping on second base to end the threat.

Winnipeg mounted its first real scoring chance in the bottom of the fourteenth when its second-sacker Brazil legged out a perfect bunt with one away. Arthur Henning, Maroon first baseman and league batting champ, followed with a long double to the alley in centre field. "Chief" Williams had a slight problem fielding the ball and Sheehan, coaching at third, waved Brazil home, but Williams found the handle on the ball in time to whistle a peg to the plate well in advance of the runner. Brazil attempted to bowl Byers over and dislodge the ball but to no avail.

A weary Leo Seiffert took to the mound for the start of the eighteenth inning. A lapse in judgement caused him to play a sacrifice bunt to first base when there was ample time to get the runner at second. Brazil, covering the bag at first, threw wildly to second base in his hurry to try for the double play. Instead of two routine outs the Quakers had a runner on third base and only one out. Williams drew another intentional walk to set up a double-play opportunity but this time the Maroons' luck had run out. Saskatoon's first-sacker Tiffany drilled a line drive over left-fielder Gus Purpura's head, scoring both runners. A single by catcher Byers increased the Quakers' lead to three. There would be no miracle finish in the bottom of the eighteenth as Stevenson calmly retired the side to preserve his shutout.

Manitoba Free Press sportswriter W. J. Finlay called it the finest game ever played in western Canada. Saskatoon closed out the best-of-nine series by a 5-3 margin, with Stevenson pitching the series-clinching eighth contest. The championship series was considered a great success both on the diamond and at the turnstiles. Each Quaker player pocketed an extra two hundred dollars from his share of the playoff pool while the losers settled for one hundred and fifty.

In today's game David Cone has a well-deserved reputation as a hired gun, a free agent whose pitching talents are available to any contender for the right price. But Cone's four-team résumé would pale in comparison to that of Satchel Paige, the all-time champion ballplayer for hire. In 1934, when the Pittsburgh Crawfords' owner Gus Greenlee tired of "Satch" living out of his hip pocket, Paige bolted to Bismarck, North Dakota, to play for local auto-dealer Neil Campbell's semipro club. The signing of Paige broke the North Dakota colour barrier and he was soon joined by five other black players, including the talented Quincy Troupe and Ted "Double Duty" Radcliffe.

The Bismarck nine came to Winnipeg in early June of 1935 to play a four-game exhibition series with the Kansas City Monarchs at Osborne Stadium. This was a wonderful Monarch line-up that included Bullet Joe Rogan, arguably one of Paige's predecessors as the greatest pitcher in the Negro Leagues. Bullet Joe was more than just a pitcher, batting clean-up and patrolling the outfield in games in which he wasn't on the mound. Monarch shortstop Willard Brown was one of the most-feared power hitters in the Negro Leagues. He was the first black player to hit a home run in the American League during a brief stint with the St. Louis Browns in 1947.

The opening contest of the series pitted Paige against the Monarchs' fine young fireballer Chet Brewer. "Snake" Siddle, one of Manitoba's finest ballplayers and a veteran of the barnstorming wars with the House of David, was calling the balls and strikes. Bismarck threatened in the top of the first inning behind the hitting prowess of two of its new black recruits. Troupe lined a two-out single and was followed by Red Haley's resounding ground-rule double that caromed off the Amphitheatre hockey rink. Brewer was immune to the pressure, calmly retiring the next batter.

Paige fanned the side in the first frame, breezing through the next four innings allowing only two hits. Monarch right-fielder Taylor opened the sixth inning with a single and promptly stole second. Kansas City catcher Young hit a two-out flare that moved Taylor to third. Ever the showman, Paige intentionally walked the next batter to heighten the drama before nonchalantly fanning Brown on three straight pitches.

The Monarchs threatened again in the seventh inning when their third baseman Howard ripped a one-out triple. Brewer came to the plate with a chance to give himself the lead. Bismarck, knowing that the Negro League teams played a running game and Howard would be moving on contact, brought the infield in a few steps for a play at the plate. Brewer hit a chopper to short that Leary fielded cleanly, gunning a perfect peg to Troupe to nail the runner at home. Brewer paid for his aggressiveness when Troupe alertly applied the tag and came up throwing, erasing him at second base.

It was Brewer's turn for a little grandstanding in the top of the eighth inning. With Bismarck runners at first and second and two out, Chet intentionally walked the bases full before coolly whiffing Drengburg to end the frame. The Monarchs managed to get a runner as far as second base in the bottom of the ninth but Paige struck out the next two batters to end the threat. Only dimming sunlight could have taken the lustre out of this classic battle. Siddle called the game a scoreless draw after nine innings. In all, the fans were treated to thirty strikeouts, with Paige earning the nod 17-13.

Paige and his integrated nine went on to capture the National Baseball Congress Tournament held in Wichita that year. Some of Satch's teammates might have objected to his colour but not the 18-0 mark he posted for Bismarck that season.

The notion that semipro ball was in any way inferior to the affiliated professional leagues was put to the test any time two rival Man Dak League clubs took to the field. While the emerging black stars were eagerly drafted into major-league organizations, the Negro Leagues were steadily faltering. The early 1950s witnessed the arrival of several elite black players in Manitoba. When the Brandon Greys squared off against the Winnipeg Buffaloes for the 1950 Man Dak championship, the rosters read like a clash between the Birmingham Black Barons and the Chicago American Giants from 1946. The only white ballplayers on the field were Brandon's home-grown stars, left-fielder Gerry Mackay and third baseman Ian Lowe.

"Man Dak Champs"
The 1950 Winnipeg Buffaloes, Man Dak League champions.

The Buffaloes were coached by their hard-hitting shortstop Willie "Devil" Wells, who had his club a single road victory away from the title. Former Newark Eagle great Leon Day was on the hill for the Buffaloes, while the Greys countered with Manuel Godinez, late of the Indiannapolis Clowns. The contest was a pitchers' duel, with neither man allowing a run through regulation time. Both clubs threatened to break the game open several times but a fine running grab by Mackay in the top of the fifth inning prevented a potential run. Brandon loaded the bases in the eighth inning but Day managed to induce two inning-ending fly balls.

The tenth frame brought some real fireworks, culminating with Wells being ejected from the game under police escort. The inning opened innocently enough with a walk to Godinez, who was promptly sacrificed to second base. It appeared Day was beginning to tire when he walked Vasquez. Chuck Wilson followed with a smash back to the box that Day fielded for what should have been a tailor-made double play. However, base umpire Ray Hedley called Vasquez safe on the play at second base, causing Wells to live up to his Devil nickname. Willie refused to leave the diamond after Hedley threw him out of the game; finally umpire-in-chief Mark Van Buren gave Wells two minutes to clear off or risk a forfeit. Wells stomped out of the stadium, watching the rest of the game perched on top of Winnipeg's team bus parked directly in front of Kinsmen Memorial Park.

When order was restored the Greys had the bases loaded with only one out. Fortunately for Winnipeg, Godinez made a grievous base-running error, attempting to steal home with the dangerous clean-up hitter Rafe Cabrera at the plate. Day anticipated his mound rival's long lead off third base and called for a pitch-out. Godinez was dead meat at the plate, and the blunder unsettled Cabrera enough that he popped out to end the inning.

The Greys threatened again in the bottom of the fourteenth inning. With Mackay perched on second, Skeeter Watkins spanked a hard shot over second base. If the ball had cleared the infield the winning run would have scored, but Winnipeg's nimble second baseman Johnny Kennedy hustled to his left, speared the ball, and in one motion threw a dart to the plate. Frazier Robinson slapped the tag on Mackay, forcing the contest to continue.

Great defensive plays were becoming routine that afternoon. Mackay turned a somersault in a lunging stab, stealing an extra base hit from Robinson. Godinez flashed gold glove credentials, handling nine hot smashes back through the box. Day had clearly caught his second wind as he fanned the side in the bottom of the sixteenth. For his part, Godinez had yet to offer a base on balls. In the top of the seventeenth Butch Davis lined a ball into right field for a base hit; rounding the bag he noticed a slight hesitation by Charlie Peet and hustled in to second base. Lyman Bostock followed with a perfect sacrifice bunt, moving the tie-breaking run ninety feet from home plate. Day rolled out weakly to Godinez but a single from Joe Taylor plated the game's first run. It was all the lead that Day would require. The man who had out-duelled Ewing Blackwell before fifty thousand servicemen in a military championship in Germany knew something about pressure pitching. He calmly quieted the Greys' bats in the bottom of the seventeenth to give Winnipeg its lone Man Dak title.

Personally I've always been a big fan of the great defensive play. What is more thrilling than a diving catch or a bullet peg from the outfield for a close play at the plate? Winnipeg fans witnessed a breath-taking display of defensive wizardry in the opening contest of the Goldeyes' semifinal series in 1954. It was Winnipeg's first year back in the Northern League, with the club battling to a third-place finish and a date in the postseason. However, they were in tough, facing the pennant-winning Fargo-Moorhead. The Twins had outfielder Frank Gravino fresh off a second consecutive MVP season and the league's best pitcher in Jim "Mudcat" Grant.

Winnipeg trotted out its sixteen-game winner Bill Smith, who practically owned the Twins, having beaten them six times during the regular season. When Winnipeg scratched out a run in the bottom of the fifth inning against Fargo starter Clarence (Pete) Peerenboom, it looked like it might stand up as the game winner. In the top of the eighth inning Dick Zuccato led off with a clean poke to centre, followed up by a pair of seeing-eye singles from Steve Jankowski and Mitch June that knotted the score at ones. The game was still deadlocked after regulation.

Fargo scored two runs in the top of the tenth inning, leaving thirty-five hundred Winnipeg supporters pulling for a miracle finish. The Goldeyes weren't going down without a fight. Catcher Dahms worked Peerenboom for a base on balls and Spiller singled, pinch-hitting for Bill Smith. The crowd was up on their feet when an errant pick-off throw from Peerenboom advanced the runners to second and third. Goldeye third baseman Bill Silverthorne stepped to the plate with the tying runs in scoring position and only one away. He worked the count to three balls and a strike, guaranteeing a decent pitch to hit or a walk to load the bases. The pitch was down the middle of the plate and Silverthorne teed off on it. Twin centre-fielder Lou Krantz was off at the crack of the bat, managing to reach the base of the fence at the precise moment the ball did. Forgetting all thought for his personal safety, Krantz launched himself headlong into the fence. Fortunately the fixture was not permanently anchored because with the impact the structure moved back three feet. Despite the jarring collision Krantz had the composure to thrust his glove over the fence, somehow coming down with the ball. He did a pathetic pirouette and collapsed after making a feeble attempt at getting the ball back into the infield.

Upon Silverthorne's bat making contact with the ball, the base paths were awash with activity: Dahms and Spiller both broke for home at top speed. Gravino alertly sprinted over from his left-field position to retrieve the ball, and his relay throw to Jankowski was in time to double Spiller off second base. Dahms had had time to retrace his steps and tag up to score Winnipeg's second run but it was incidental. In one heroic effort Krantz had literally stolen a 4-3 victory away from the Goldeyes. The Twins rushed to their still-prone teammate. The first words out of his mouth were, "Did I get the guy at second?"

Goldeye manager Mickey O'Neil and his Twin counterpart Phil Seghi claimed to have never seen a more thrilling play. It turned out to be an important victory for Fargo as the Goldeyes pushed the series to its three-game limit. The Twins had an easier time, dispatching the Eau Claire Braves in two straight games to win the league championship.

In 1954 the Saskatoon Gems were growing weary of their role as perpetual bridesmaids in their competitions with the North Battleford Beavers for the Western Canada League championship. For the past three years the two teams had met in the finals, with the Beavers prevailing every year. It appeared that the Gems had extracted a modicum of revenge when they captured the seventh and deciding game of the series, but the celebration proved premature when the league stepped in to uphold an earlier Beaver protest that Saskatoon used an ineligible player. A sudden-death finale was played on September 9 at Saskatoon's Cairns Field before a packed house of over four thousand fans.

The Beavers' choice to pitch this all-important contest was Jackie McLeod. The team was fortunate that Jackie was not one to hold a grudge. Earlier that summer he had been fired as the club's playing manager, only rejoining the Beavers for the final three games of the championship series. Saskatoon had flown Don Kirk in from Edmonton to handle its mound duties.

North Battleford catcher Lou Green drove in the game's first run in the top of the second inning. The Beavers added to their lead when Green worked Kirk for a bases-loaded walk in the sixth frame, adding a third run on a passed ball by catcher Bob Bennett.

Saskatoon roared back in the bottom of the sixth, when two walks sandwiched around a single by Mario Herrera loaded the sacks. Max Bentley, a pretty fair hockey player in his spare time, laced a shot to right-centre that scored two runs. In a heads-up bit of base running he took second base on the throw-in, moving the go-ahead run into scoring position with nobody out. McLeod dug a little deeper, fanning the next three hitters to end the threat. Saskatoon could not mount another offensive and North Battleford had its fourth consecutive championship, thanks in large part to a man whom management had felt was expendable six weeks earlier. The little southpaw went the distance, striking out ten Saskatoon batters.

The following season McLeod was in a Gems uniform as the team faced the Regina Braves in the seventh game of the semifinals. Jackie continued his penchant for the dramatic by scoring the winning run in the bottom of the ninth inning. Eleven years later, he attempted to instil some of his winning attitude into Canada's National Hockey Team after replacing Father David Bauer as the club's coach and general manager.

In 1957 the Edmonton Eskimos captured the Western Canada League championship with a six-game triumph over the Moose Jaw Mallards, earning the right to represent Canada at the Global World Series being held in Briggs Stadium (now Tiger Stadium) in Detroit. Semipro clubs from all over the world met to contest this annual event. Owing to a rigorous time constraint, tournament rules banned all infield or batting practice before games.

Edmonton ousted Venezuela 5-1 in the semifinals behind the three-hit pitching of Ernie Nevers to advance to the finals against Japan. The

EDMONTON ESKIMOS
Western Canada Baseball League, 1957

Left to Right—JOE RINEY, O.F.; CON MUNATONES, O.F.; MIKE MICHAELS, C.; KEN GUFFEY, 1B.; RON FAIRLY, O.F.; WAYNE TUCKER, Mgr., 2B.; TOM SHOLLIN, C.; MIKE CASTANON, Inf.; MIKE BLEWETT, Inf.

Second Row—DICK BIELOUS, Trainer; DALE ZEIGLER, P.; BLAINE SYLVESTER, P.; LARRY ELLIOTT, P.-O.F.; STEVE EVANS, P.; BRUCE MONT-GOMERY, P.; ED SADA, Inf.; RALPH VOLD, P.; JOHN DUCEY, Gen. Mgr.

Sitting in front—JIM MONAHAN, Bat Boy.

"Global Championship Runners-up"
The Edmonton Eskimos won the Western Canada Baseball League championship in 1957 and finished second to Japan in the Global Championships played at Detroit's Tiger Stadium.

two clubs had met in the opening game of the tournament, with Japan capturing a 3-2 victory in thirteen innings.

The Esks' lone Canadian player, Ralph Void, was given the starting assignment in the final contest. Void had not pitched in five days but showed no ill effects from the no-warm-up rule. He cruised through the first six innings, staked to a one-run lead on a run-scoring single by shortstop Ed Sada. In the bottom of the sixth Ron Fairly snapped out of a prolonged hitting slump by depositing a solo homer over the short right-field porch.

Japan's fortunes took a turn for the better after its compact five-foot-five-inch and 130-pound captain Sadoyoshi Osawa was inserted into the line-up in the sixth inning. Osawa stung Void for a one-out solo blast in the top of the seventh inning, but he was only getting warmed up. Edmonton clung to a narrow 2-1 margin with two out and a runner on second when Osawa next strode to the plate. He worked the count to two balls and two strikes before drilling a ball to the wall in left-centre to deadlock the contest. Nevers came on to replace Void and retired the side.

Osawa proved to be a handy man with a glove, grabbing Sada's long drive to left-centre in the bottom of the tenth, preventing the winning run from scoring. In his next plate appearance Osawa worked Edmonton's third hurler of the day, Mike Blewett, for a walk to start the eleventh inning. The next batter popped out but Blewett served up a free pass to Jitsuo. Osawa's dancing off of second base flustered the Esks pitcher into a balk ball, placing both runners in scoring position. Masayuki Furata salted away a Japanese victory with a two-run single back through the middle. The Esks had one final shot in the bottom of the eleventh but could not solve Tukashi Sazuke's tantalizing curve ball.

When interviewed for the 1994 Edmonton Trappers program, Ron Fairly fondly reminisced about his year in Edmonton. The Esks were given a set of commemorative silver cufflinks by the Province of Alberta that Fairly still owned.

I can in no way claim that these were the six greatest games ever played on the Prairies. They do, however, provide an overview of some of the thrilling encounters that took place. A game that comes to mind from my own personal recollection pitted the Northern League all-stars against the Minnesota Twins in 1964. This was a talented Twin line-up only one year away from the club's first-ever trip to the World Series. Dave Boswell of Bismarck made the big leaguers look like amateurs by fanning six men in three innings' work as the Northern Leaguers defeated the Twins 5-2. Boswell is perhaps better remembered for another piece of Minnesota baseball history: he was unlucky enough to have his jaw broken by a sucker punch from his manager Billy Martin in 1969.

LEGENDS OF
THE PRAIRIES

CHOOSING AN ALL-STAR TEAM FROM THE MANY SKILLED BALLPLAYERS TO PLY their talents on the Prairies since the turn of the century is a daunting task. In fairness I have chosen only those players who went on to attain the pinnacle of the profession. In certain instances skin colour prevented some of my choices from playing in the major leagues, but the three players in question were among the elite in Negro League baseball history. My second criterion was that the players had played on the Prairies for at least a season and were not part of a touring club. Grover Cleveland Alexander, Lefty Grove, Jimmie Foxx, Satchel Paige, and "Cool Papa" Bell are but a few of the superstars who made stopovers on the Prairies while barnstorming. Players of a more recent vintage who played a portion of a season but did not qualify for the all-star team are Edmonton Trapper pitchers Bert Blyleven and Fernando Valenzuela.

Local Talent
Having made major-league status a criterion for making my club, it would be remiss to not mention some of the fine local talent that toiled in relative obscurity. While lacking the hype of today's two-sport athletes like Jordan and Jackson, several National Hockey League players were

"Fernando, You Look Mahvelous"
The great Fernando Valenzuela pitching for Edmonton in 1991.

excellent baseball players. Terry Sawchuk might have been the N.H.L.'s shutout king, but he broke up many a pitcher's shutout with his booming bat while playing first base for the Elmwood Giants of the Manitoba League in 1948; and Leroy Goldsworthy of the Detroit Red Wings was the "ace" of the Winnipeg Maroons' pitching staff during the mid-thirties.

In Saskatchewan Jackie McLeod, player-coach of Canada's National Hockey Team in the mid-sixties and early seventies, starred for several clubs in the W.C.L. a decade earlier. Among his teammates while at North Battleford was Emile "the Cat" Francis, long-time general manager of the New York Rangers. Doug and Max Bentley, along with two of their brothers, fronted the Delisle Tigers, a force to be reckoned with in any cash tournament played in Saskatchewan. In Alberta, Jim "Tiny" Thompson, the great Boston netminder, won a gold watch and chain for leading the Calgary Senior League in hitting in 1924.

Other talented ballplayers, who didn't lace on skates in the winter, included Winnipeg's "Snake" Siddle, good enough to tour with the House of David during the twenties. Hugh Gustafson, the slugging first baseman of the Winnipeg Maroons in the late thirties, moved up the professional ranks to play Class B ball at Moline of Triple I League. Ian Lowe and Gerry Mackay were mainstays on the Brandon Greys during their successful sojourn in the Man Dak League. Gayle Shupe was one of the top hurlers in Saskatchewan after leading the Northern League in wins with Winnipeg in 1939. Dodger Lewis was one of Alberta's finest hurlers in the twenties and thirties, forming a battery with his hard-hitting brother, Frank. The "Lewis Boys" hired out their services to teams throughout Alberta and Saskatchewan.

The All-Star Roster

The all-star roster will contain two players at each position and provide for a D.H. for those pure hitters who were a little suspect with the leather.

Ted "Double Duty" Radcliffe had twenty-three years of service with the Negro Leagues when he signed on to be the playing manager of the Elmwood Giants of the Man Dak League in 1951. Theodore Roosevelt Radcliffe owed his "Double Duty" moniker to Damon Runyon, who coined the nickname after watching Ted catch Satchel Paige in a 5-0 shutout in the first game of a double-header, then come back to pitch a shutout himself in the second game. Radcliffe was the master of the emery ball and other dubious deliveries, making him a selection at catcher alone. In 1935, he was part of the integrated Bismarck squad that captured the national semipro championship at Wichita. He was a career .280 hitter who handled Paige for four of his no-hitters. In 1945 he roomed with Jackie Robinson while playing for the Kansas City Monarchs. He was greatly impressed by the respect Robinson showed to his elders and the fans and was not surprised when the Brooklyn Dodgers chose Jackie as the first black player to integrate the majors. Radcliffe was well past his prime when he played for Elmwood but the box scores still indicate that he could swing the bat.

Unlike Radcliffe, Tom Haller's baseball career was just beginning when he caught for the Moose Jaw Mallards in 1957. There were no roadblocks impeding Haller's path to the big leagues; instead he had to choose between returning to the University of Illinois to quarterback the football team or signing a $50,000-bonus baby contract with the New York Giants baseball club. He opted for baseball, joining the Mallards at the end of the college year. By 1962 he had graduated to the San Francisco Giants, where his eighteen home runs helped the refugees from the Polo Grounds attain their first West Coast trip to the World Series. Haller distinguished himself by blasting a two-run homer off Whitey Ford in the fourth game of the fall classic. He has the distinction of catching all twenty-three innings in a Giants-Mets marathon contest. Haller moved over to the American League in 1972; in one contest as a Detroit Tiger the man directly behind him calling the balls and strikes was his brother Bill. He ended an eleven-year career with a .257 batting average and 134 home runs.

When the Winnipeg Maroons captured the Northern Copper League championship in 1907, Fred Luderus was their first-sacker. Along with teammate Rollie Zeider, Luderus was among the earliest Prairie alumni to graduate to the "show." Two years later Luderus led the Wisconsin-Illinois circuit in hitting, prompting a call up to the Chicago Cubs late in the season. A trade to the Philadelphia Phillies marked the beginning of a prolific ten years. Despite the "dead ball" era, Luderus cracked sixteen home runs in 1911, batting fifth behind slugger Gavvy Gravath; the pair owned the short right-field porch in Philadelphia's Baker Bowl. He was the first Philly to park two homers in one game. In 1915 the Phillies advanced to the World Series, with Luderus hitting at a .315 clip, finishing second for the league batting title. Despite Philadelphia bowing out in five games to the Boston Red Sox, Luderus hit a robust .438 with a team-leading six runs batted in. He was a durable performer, reeling off 533 consecutive games played between 1916 and 1919, while boasting that he was never removed for a pinch-hitter.

Ron Fairly came right off the campus of the University of Southern California to join the Edmonton Eskimos in 1957. Esks general manager John Ducey was a friend of Trojan coach Rod Dedeaux, recruiting both Fairly and later pitcher Pat Gillick for his semipro club. Fairly was an immediate hit with Edmonton fans, helping to carry the club to a league championship and a very creditable second-place finish in the Global World Series. The following year at the age of nineteen, he debuted with the Los Angeles Dodgers. He remained a backup outfielder with the club until 1962, when moving to first place solidified his spot on the starting roster. He paced the club with two home runs and six runs batted in during the Dodgers' thrilling seven-game World Series victory over Minnesota in 1965. In 1969 Fairly was traded to the expansion Montreal Expos, where he put up some of his best power numbers in the hitter-friendly confines of Jarry Park. The Toronto Blue Jays acquired the classy veteran for their inaugural campaign in 1977, and he responded with a career-high nineteen home runs en route to a berth on the all-star team. Fairly finished his twenty-one-year major-league career with 215 homers and over a thousand RBIs.

Oscar Mellilo was the second baseman for the Winnipeg Maroons in 1921, the final year of operation for that incarnation of the W.C.L. The circuit was at its most competitive that season as several players, including Mellilo and his teammate pitcher Tony Kaufman, graduated to the majors. Oscar suffered from Bright's disease and was nicknamed "Spinach" after doctors ordered that the green vegetable become a staple in his diet. Mellilo debuted with the St. Louis Browns in 1926, spending a decade toiling with perennial non-contenders. He was a quality run producer for a middle infielder, averaging better than sixty-five RBIs a season between 1929 and 1934. While he didn't play on great teams, he certainly came in contact with two of the greatest second basemen of all time. Rogers Hornsby was the Browns' manager during Mellilo's final season in St. Louis; moving over to the Boston Red Sox, Mellilo helped tutor young Bobby Doerr in the intricacies of second base.

If athletic ability is an inherent trait, then Bret Boone had an unfair advantage over his competitors. Boone's grandfather Ray was a major-league shortstop and third baseman for thirteen seasons. Bret's dad Bob owned the record for the most games played by a catcher until it was broken by Carlton Fisk in 1993. Bret was a can't-miss prospect with the Calgary Cannons in 1992, making the all-star team, hitting for power, and stealing bases. Failing to crack the starting line-up in Seattle the following year, he returned to the friendly confines of Foothills Stadium to hit .332. Desperate for relief pitching, the Mariners traded Boone to the Cincinnati Reds in 1994, where he responded by hitting .320 in his first complete major-league season. Boone's batting average slipped slightly in 1995 but his power totals increased. In the not-too-distant future it is possible that Boone will be mentioned with Robbie Alomar and Carlos Baerga among the elite players at his position.

"Boone Tries to Turn Two"
Bret Boone makes the pivot
and fires over to first in a
1993 contest at Foothills
Stadium.

The choice at shortstop is made somewhat more difficult by the fact that Danny Tartabull was the Pacific Coast League MVP while playing the position for Calgary in 1985. Tartabull has crafted some strong power numbers over the past decade but mainly as an outfielder and D.H. Unfortunately his career has been derailed by injuries and a stint in Steinbreiner's "Bronx Zoo" of late.

Willie Wells was on the downside of a brilliant career in the Negro Leagues when he signed on to manage and play for the Winnipeg Buffaloes of the Man Dak League in 1950. He ranks among the top six home-run hitters in Negro League history. While lacking Josh Gibson's reputation as a slugger, Wells holds the record for the most home runs in a season with twenty-seven round-trippers. He was not blessed with a cannon for an arm, instead using an uncanny ability of knowing where to play the hitters to get the job done. Wells was chosen to play in the East-West all-star game eight times.

"Devil," as he was known, was part of the Newark Eagles' "million dollar infield" in the late thirties. He was a strong proponent of playing in Latin America, feeling that there a man was judged on merit and not the colour of his skin. Wells was notorious for being hit by pitches and is credited with fashioning one of the earliest batting helmets by knocking the gas jet off an old miner's helmet. In his many travels, Wells hit .328 in the Negro Leagues, .320 in seven winters in Cuba, .378 in Puerto Rico, and .392 while competing against major leaguers in exhibition contests.

The 1920 Moose Jaw Millers had a little shortstop in Mark Koenig. Playing with the New York Yankees in 1926, Koenig and Tony Lazzeri made baseball history, becoming the only rookie double-play combo to lead a team to the World Series. Koenig failed to distinguish himself in that series but rebounded with nine hits the following year when the Yanks routed the Pittsburgh Pirates. A year later, he hit a sizzling .319 during the regular season as the Bronx Bombers repeated as world champions. Koenig was very well liked by his Yankee teammates, placing him at the centre of a World Series controversy in 1932. He had been demoted to the minors by the Detroit Tigers that season, only to have his contract purchased by the Chicago Cubs in August. Koenig hit a torrid .353 for the Cubbies down the stretch drive to help them win the pennant. However, his late-season heroics were overlooked when the Cubs voted him a half share in the World Series pool. Babe Ruth was livid upon hearing about the tight-fisted manner in which his pal had been treated. Before the opening game of the World Series, he led a delegation of Yanks over to the Cub dugout to berate the chisellers. Bench jockeying hit new lows in that series with Ruth oinking like a pig at the Cub bench as he trotted around the bases following his famous "called shot" off Charley Root.

Koenig's final trip to the World Series was with the New York Giants in 1936. In all he played in five fall classics with three different teams, while batting a respectable .279 over his twelve-year career.

While the choice for all the other infield positions was very difficult, there has been a dearth of quality Prairie third-base alumni. An argument could be made for the 1907 Winnipeg Maroons' Rollie Zeider. Dubbed "Bunions" after contracting blood poisoning from a Ty Cobb spiking, Zeider was only a .240 hitter over a seven-year career with the Cubs and White Sox. However, his forty-nine steals in his rookie season would provide a rare commodity in speed from the hot corner.

The most obvious choice for third sack would be Edgar Martinez, not only for his prowess with the bat but for his longevity on the Canadian plains. He played portions of four seasons with the Calgary Cannons before finally getting a legitimate shot with the Seattle Mariners. He won a Pacific Coast League batting title in 1988, duplicating the feat four years later in Seattle. At the age of thirty, it appeared that Martinez's career was finally going to take off. Unfortunately he suffered a torn hamstring on a wet field in Vancouver during the Mariners' final exhibition series of the 1993 season. The injury was serious enough to write off the entire season. The following year he was hit on the wrist with a pitch, limiting his playing time to eighty-nine games. Martinez played winter ball in his native Puerto Rico, returning to the Mariner line-up healthy for the first time in two seasons. His hard work and perseverance are being rewarded with an inspired performance. He captured his second batting title while posting career highs in home runs and RBIs. Edgar drove in the game-winning run in the fifth and deciding game of the wild-card-series contest against the New York Yankees. Along with teammates Ken Griffey Jr. and Jay Buhner, Martinez served notice that the once lamentable Mariners are a force to be reckoned with. His late-season heroics are a major factor in the Seattle City Council voting in favour of building a new ballpark to keep the team.

The choice of an all-time outfield was perhaps the most difficult, since there were some outstanding candidates to choose from. Kenny Williams had the distinction of playing for two Western Canada League teams. In 1913 he patrolled the outfield for the Regina Red Sox, returning the following year to play with the Edmonton Gray Birds. The second season displayed some of his speed as he stole forty-two bases. Williams fit right in with the small-town atmosphere that prevailed in the W.C.L., having been raised in tiny Grants Pass, Oregon, where his mother was a logging-camp cook.

He debuted in the "bigs" in 1915 with Cincinnati before moving over to the St. Louis Browns in 1919. The Browns' outfield consisting of "Baby Doll" Jacobson, Jack Tobin and Williams is considered to be among the best ever. Williams was often overshadowed by the hitting exploits of his teammate George Sisler but he did manage to produce one monster season that gained him league-wide recognition. It was 1922 and an ailing Babe Ruth surrendered the home-run crown to Williams. Williams' numbers for that season are an eye-popping .332 batting average, league-best thirty-nine homers, and 155 runs batted in. He also managed to steal thirty-seven bases, becoming the first member of the elite thirty-thirty club. He retired after thirteen seasons, sporting a sparkling .319 batting average.

Heinie Manush topped the W.C.L. in 1921 by hitting nine homers for the Edmonton Eskimos. By 1923 Manush was in the Detroit Tigers' outfield alongside Ty Cobb and Harry Heilman. The two Tiger future Hall of Famers found an eager pupil in Heinie. In 1926 Manush went six for nine during a season-ending double-header to out-duel Babe Ruth for the batting title. Two years later he batted .378 for the lowly St. Louis Browns, only to lose the batting crown by a point.

Manush was a line-drive hitter with enough speed to leg out 163 triples. He batted .330 over a seventeen-year career and is enshrined in the Hall of Fame.

The Edmonton Trappers' Tim Salmon served notice that he was a player to be reckoned with by leading the Pacific Coast League in home runs and runs batted in en route to capturing *Baseball America*'s Minor League Player of the Year in 1992. He made the transition to the majors look effortless, capturing the American League Rookie of the Year with the California Angels the following year. Salmon's numbers dipped slightly in his sophomore season but much of that can be blamed on a bad team. In 1995 the Angels were one of baseball's most pleasant surprises. Talented young players like Jim Edmonds and Garrett Anderson have moved alongside Salmon to provide the Angels with one of the game's most exciting outfields. With the added pop in California's line-up, opposing pitchers will no longer be able to pitch around Salmon, and this should allow him to produce some staggering numbers.

Much has been made of Mickey Mantle's struggle to endure crippling knee injuries to perform at an elite level. Andre Dawson has struggled with the same problems while playing his career outside of the media circus in New York. Dawson led the Pioneer League in homers with the Lethbridge Expos during their inaugural year in 1975. He had all the tools: power, speed, and a wonderful throwing arm. Watching him play was like seeing Bobby Orr: the guy has all the talent in the world but has literally played his entire career on one good leg.

My final three outfielders are better known for their prowess with the bat than for their glove work, making them useful in the role of designated hitter. Jake Fournier led the W.C.L. in hits and runs scored while playing for the Moose Jaw Robin Hoods in 1911. The following year Fournier cracked the Chicago White Sox line-up, but four years later he was demoted to the minors despite hitting well over .300. Sox manager "Pants" Rowland felt that there was a defensive component to baseball and hoped that a little more seasoning in the minors would turn Fournier into a complete ballplayer. The experiment was a failure; practice did not necessarily make perfect in Jake's case. Ultimately the more lively ball made popular in the early twenties salvaged Fournier's major-league career. He developed into a feared slugger with the Brooklyn Dodgers, averaging better than twenty homers and one hundred runs driven in from 1923 to 1925. Fournier had enough speed to swipe 145 bases while batting .313 over a fifteen-year career.

The Edmonton Trappers' Ron Kittle put up some Ruthian numbers en route to being voted *Baseball America's* and *Sporting News'* Minor League Player of the Year in 1982. Big Ron smashed fifty homers and drove in 144 runs for the Trappers that season. Just to prove it was no fluke, he hit thirty-five for the Chicago White Sox the following year, capturing the American League Rookie of the Year honours. Kittle had serious power, often launching tape-measure shots when he connected. Unfortunately a .239 batting average limited his big-league career to only ten seasons.

Floyd Caves "Babe" Herman led the W.C.L. in hits while playing for the Edmonton Eskimos in 1921. By 1926 he was a regular in the outfield of the Brooklyn Dodgers and, to quote Rodney Dangerfield, "getting no respect." The man had a career batting average of .324 but the press insisted on portraying him as a simpleton. He hit .393 in 1930 only to lose the batting title to Bill Terry's .401, but still the press chose to concentrate on his fielding shortcomings and base-path blunders. There is one famous story of how he played a fly ball off his head and another about how he tripled into a triple play. I've witnessed Jose Canseco play a ball off his head that caromed over the fence for a home run and I'm certain that it will not be his epitaph. The triple-play story was simply a case of aggressive base running on Herman's part. The Dodgers had runners at first and third when Herman hit a long fly ball.

The runner on third chose to admire it while the runner on first raced around the bases, barely ahead of Babe. As a result all three men ended up on third base when the ball was relayed back into the infield. The rival third baseman tagged all three runners, stating "One of you sons of bitches is out."

Herman was a part of baseball history when he homered in the first-ever night contest played in Cincinnati.

Give me this group of hitters and I'd feel confident competing against any of today's clubs.

The Prairies were proving grounds for some outstanding pitchers over the years. To that end I have chosen a starting rotation of four pitchers, using a southpaw-righty combination.

My fourth starter would be southpaw Ray Sadecki, who started his minor-league career as a seventeen-year-old with the Winnipeg Goldeyes in 1958. Two years later, he won nine games while still a teenager pitching for the St. Louis Cardinals. In 1964 he won twenty games to help the Cardinals make it into the World Series. Sadecki got the start in game one ahead of Bob Gibson, escaping with a 9-5 victory over the Yankees. Gibson went on to win three games in the Cards' seven-game triumph, establishing himself as one of baseball's dominant pitchers, but Sadecki was a vital cog in getting the Cards there.

Sadecki's next postseason experience would come nine years later as a reliever with the New York Mets. He came out of the bull pen four times during the seven-game series, recording a save and posting a sparkling 1.93 ERA. Ray pitched for eighteen years in the major leagues, ending up with a 135-131 record and seven saves.

In 1963, Nelson Briles was the staff ace of the Calgary Giants of the cash-strapped Western Canada League. Two years later, he was in the bull pen of the St. Louis Cardinals. In 1967, Briles moved into the starting rotation after Bob Gibson had his leg broken by a Roberto Clemente liner. Briles was an impressive 14-5 in helping the Cards into the World Series. He won the third game of the series, going the route on a 5-2 victory. The following season, Briles chipped in with nineteen wins as the Cards returned to the postseason.

Briles was the definitive big-game player: although no longer a dominant pitcher, he came on to toss the all-important fifth game for Pittsburgh in the 1971 World Series. Briles out-duelled Baltimore Oriole ace Dave McNally for a 4-0 shutout. His 129-112 mark with twenty-two saves makes him a worthy addition to the starting rotation.

It would be difficult to pick a number-one starter on this team because both of the remaining pitchers are Hall of Famers. The staff's second right-hander, Leon Day pitched for the Man Dak-champion Winnipeg Buffaloes in 1950. Day was no stranger to Canadian diamonds, pitching for the Toronto Maple Leafs of the International League the following year and the Edmonton Eskimos of the Western International circuit in 1953.

Leon Day ranks among the greatest pitchers of the Negro Leagues. A wonderful all-around athlete, he could play any position on the diamond except catcher. He was 13-0 pitching for the Newark Eagles in 1937, while still managing to hit .320 as a position player. He eclipsed Satchel Paige's record for strikeouts in a single game by fanning eighteen hitters in a contest in 1942. Three years later, while in the military, he defeated major-leaguer Ewell Blackwell for the European Service Championship before fifty thousand cheering GIs in Nuremburg. He tossed a no-hitter for Newark his first game back from the services. Unfortunately, by the time Jackie Robinson integrated the majors, Day was considered too old to be a prospect. Still, the Hall of Fame welcomed him to the fold in 1995.

Winnipeg Goldeyes fans didn't realize it at the time but they had a phenomenon in their midst in 1964. Steve "Lefty" Carlton only posted a 4-4 mark that season; however, by the time his twenty-four-year sojourn in the "bigs" was over, he would amass 329 victories and rank second on the list behind Nolan Ryan for career strikeouts. Carlton is the only pitcher to win the Cy Young Award four times.

An inductee to the Hall of Fame in 1994, Carlton maintained a training regime that would have brought a lesser man to his knees. He ran in a trough of rice to build up his leg muscles and carried a set of steel ball-bearings to strengthen his grip. He was a practitioner of both kung fu and t'ai chi. "Lefty" was one of the first athletes to openly shun the media. The passion for privacy has diminished somewhat since his retirement, although many of his recent interviews have been at best eccentric, with some of his philosophies bordering on racism.

Mike Marshall has the rare distinction of being the only player on this team to pass through the Prairies at mid-career. He had already experienced unsuccessful tours in Detroit and Seattle when the Montreal Expos purchased his contract from Houston in July 1970, shipping him to their Triple A affiliate, the Winnipeg Whips. It would be a short stopover in Winnipeg for Marshall as he emerged as the Expos' closer before the end of the season.

Marshall held a doctorate in physiology, designing his own fitness program that called for a four-mile jog every day. His education and highbrow approach to the game intimidated many of his early managers. Montreal manager Gene Mauch had the good sense to leave him alone and Marshall flourished. In 1974, while pitching for the Los Angeles Dodgers, he became the first reliever ever to garner a Cy Young Award. His training regime must have put him in good stead that year as he appeared in a mind-boggling 106 games. Marshall is considered to be one of the game's first dominant closers.

Not a bad alumni to come out of some leagues that barely made their expenses.

IT DOESN'T GET ANY BETTER THAN THIS

ACCORDING TO LLOYD JOHNSON AND MILES WOLFF, THE EDITORS OF *The Encyclopedia of Minor League Baseball* published by Baseball America Incorporated in 1993, the minor-league game has steadily been increasing in popularity since 1978. Until the strike shortened the 1994 campaign, the same could be said for the majors. However, the fans appear to have long memories, and they stayed away from big-league parks in alarming numbers in 1995. Skyrocketing ticket prices have taken an evening at the ballpark out of the realm of affordable family entertainment for most people. This trend bodes well for the minors, where most of the parks are small and intimate with plenty of cheap seats.

The Edmonton Trappers remain a stable franchise despite having changed major-league affiliates four times in the past fifteen years. The team ended a two-year association with the Florida Marlins after 1994 to become the top farm club of the Oakland A's. The '94 campaign marked the end for venerable Ducey Park, as the facility was no longer deemed up to the Triple A standards in the new agreement with the major leagues. The Edmonton City Council voted to aid in the building of a new ten-thousand-seat stadium as part of the agreement with Peter

"A Final Look at a Baseball Shrine"
The venerable Ducey Park in its second-last year of action, 1993.

Pocklington to keep the Edmonton Oilers in town. The new park has an Astroturf infield and a grass outfield. The fans seemed to appreciate the new facility, as the Trappers established a team-record attendance mark with 426,012 supporters. Edmonton had an exciting club with Oakland's top pitching prospect Doug Johns and two PCL all-stars, catcher George Williams and shortstop Fausto Cruz.

The Calgary Cannons changed affiliates at the start of the 1995 season, moving over to the National League as the Pittsburgh Pirates' Triple A affiliate. The Cannons are always near the top in attendance in the Pacific Coast League; in 1987 they were the circuit's top draw with over 300,000 fans. The city was forced to add thirteen hundred seats behind the third-base dugout and upgrade the concessions and washrooms. In July 1994 an agreement was struck between the ball club, the City of Calgary, and the Federal Infrastructure Program to fund major renovations for Foothills Stadium.

The Cannons still managed to draw well despite having the league's worst record. A long list of injuries to the parent-club Pirates' line-up forced a revolving door of players to be shipped to Pittsburgh and prevented Calgary from establishing a set roster. However, the team did produce the classiest story to come out of baseball in a long while. The Tucson Toros' stopoff in Calgary during their final road swing turned into an expensive one. A burglar broke into their rooms, stealing all the players' money. Cannon general manager Gary Arthur took it upon himself to personally reimburse every player who filled out a police report. The thief had grabbed over a thousand dollars but Arthur felt responsible since the Cannons had chosen the visiting team's hotel. As he put it, "I know what the lost money means to minor leaguers. I'm one myself."

The Lethbridge Mounties played their fourth and final season as an independent franchise in the Pioneer League in 1995. The club has signed an agreement with the expansion Arizona Diamondbacks for the 1996 campaign. Not having the benefit of a major-league organization to provide players and defray expenses left the Mounties to rely on the innovative marketing techniques of their youthful general manager Matt Ellis. The club offered six-dollar haircuts in the stands and gave half the profits to the Canadian Cancer Society. Other unique wrinkles included an alphabetical batting order in an attempt to stop a losing streak, and "Pack Your Bags Night," when two lucky patrons won a trip to Toronto to see the Blue Jays play provided they left directly from the ballpark. They did, however, phase out the "Dynamite Lady"; her act consisted of blowing up a box with her in it.

The Medicine Hat Blue Jays had not made it to the postseason for thirteen years going into the 1995 season. It was not a matter of the Jays not having young talent in their organization. It was the fact that Toronto stocked the club with seventeen- and eighteen-year-old legitimate rookies, while other Pioneer League clubs chose older, more experienced players. The league stepped in to set age limits for players, enabling Medicine Hat to make the playoffs. The successful season was all the more sweet, considering that a flood ruined the club's ballpark before opening day. The "Baby Jays" dispatched heavily favoured Billings, the club with the league's best record, in three games to capture the Northern Division crown. Unfortunately they came up against the Helena Brewers, owners of a torrid 29-7 mark in the second half of the season, and bowed out of the finals in two straight games.

Regina and Saskatoon both bought franchises in the new North Central League in 1994, a Class A independent circuit with clubs in Huron, Marshall, Brainerd, and Minneapolis. A thirty-year hiatus from organized professional baseball in Saskatchewan came to an end when

the Regina Cyclones squared off against the Minneapolis Loons in front
of thirty-one hundred fans at Regina's Currie Field. Regina's player-
coach Jason Felice had a perfect 4-4 day at the plate, including a pair
of homers, as the Cyclones sent the hometown crowd away happy with
an 8-1 victory. The Loons had some former major-leaguers in their
line-up, including their player-manager Greg Olson and pitcher Juan
Berenguer. Olson was only two years removed from the starting catching
job with the Atlanta Braves. He was quite content to live off his
lucrative final big-league contract but had one firm demand before
signing with the Loons. Olson had to have a John Deere tractor, one of
the combined lawnmowers and snowblowers, before he would sign his
contract. Berenguer's motivation was purely to earn another crack at
the "show."

The Saskatoon Riot were less fortunate in their debut, dropping a
9-2 decision on the road to the Huron Heaters.

There were many similarities between the new North Central League
and the old W.C.L., including the inevitable financial difficulties. The
Marshall Mallards could not meet their payroll and were forced to finish
the season playing all of their home games in Brainerd. When the school
bells started ringing the Saskatoon Riot, comprised mainly of California
college players, chose to forfeit rather than replay a contest late in the
season.

Huron dropped out of the league at the end of the season. Still the
playoffs went off without a hitch. The Brainerd Bears had tried to sign
Jason Felice prior to the season. Regina had to be thankful that he chose
to play for the Cyclones; he not only managed the club, guiding it to first
place in the Northern Division, but captured the triple crown as the
league's top hitter as well. Brainerd edged Minneapolis, capturing the
Southern Division to set up a clash with Regina in the finals.

The two clubs split the first four games in the best-of-five series, with
three contests requiring extra innings. Currie Field was rocking with
4,485 spectators shoehorned into the stands to watch the rubber match.
Despite four Cyclone errors, the contest was deadlocked at four apiece
after regulation. Casey Waller singled for the Bears to start the tenth
inning, advancing to second base when Dennis Hood, the normally
reliable Cyclone shortstop, misplayed Andre Johnson's high-hopper for
his second error of the contest. Regina reliever Kevin Ehl walked the

bases full, eventually allowing the winning run to cross home plate on another base on balls. The Brainerd Bears were the inaugural North Central champs.

League president George Vedder was filled with optimism for the 1995 season. He told the *Regina Leader Post* that no fewer than thirteen groups had contacted him enquiring about franchises, including old Northern League standbys like Fargo, St. Cloud, Bismarck, and Minot. Three groups in Brandon were reportedly prepared to pay $110,000 U.S. for a franchise that had cost the original six clubs $45,000 U.S. a year earlier.

Vedder was right! There was an interest in expansion, but it didn't include him or the league-champion Brainerd Bears. He attempted to keep the North Central afloat by propping up teams in Chaska and Hibbing, Minnesota, and Joliet, Illinois, but by early July the league folded in a cloud of accusations and bounced cheques.

Minneapolis, Saskatoon, and Regina moved on to join the newly formed Prairie League in 1995. The two Saskatchewan teams were joined by the Moose Jaw Diamond Dogs and Brandon Grey Owls to form a Canadian Division. Minneapolis teamed with Minot, Aberdeen, and the Dakota Rattlers, who played out of Bismarck, to form the American Division. The league salary cap was set at $70,000 Canadian and the designated-hitter rule was in effect. The top two teams from each division made it into the postseason.

Brandon worked out an informal agreement with the Northern League's Winnipeg Goldeyes for players. The Grey Owls started the season with three Manitobans on the roster. Pitcher Vince Eastman, the oldest player on the team at twenty-seven, played the previous season for the Virden Oilers. Second baseman Jamie Waddell-Johnson was a Brandon Cloverleaf alumnus while Brandon-born third-sacker Scott Hlady joined the club from Mayville State.

The league needed to sell one thousand tickets per game to reach the break-even point. Over the first month of the season attendance was strong in Moose Jaw and Saskatoon, with Regina lagging slightly compared with the huge crowds that had attended the previous year's playoffs. The only real disappointment was in Brandon where a slow start by the club had the team averaging four hundred fans a game.

As in most lower minor leagues, club management often felt that the officials performed to a lower standard than the ballplayers. A game in Minot in late August between the Mallards and Brandon almost had to be cancelled when the league-appointed umpires refused to work the third game of a weekend series. The crew had grown weary of the antics of both teams' managers during the series. Brandon player-manager Bryan Clutterback didn't even make it into the second contest after complaining bitterly about a call from the previous night's game. Minot's player-manager Mark Hebbeler wasn't around for the end of the second game after being shown the gate in the fourth inning. There was an hour's delay until local substitute umpires stepped into the breach to call the play.

The Aberdeen Pheasants owned the first Prairie League season, finishing with an outstanding 56-13 and a minor-league-record .812 winning percentage. Pheasant players dominated the postseason awards, with first baseman Ken Tripeck capturing league MVP after hitting .393 with twenty homers and seventy-two runs driven in. Aberdeen's Darren Reichie won Pitcher of the Year with a perfect 14-0 mark and a fine 2.77 ERA. Moose Jaw captured the Canadian Division, paced by the torrid hitting of Brian Cornelius who led the circuit with a .403 batting average, a scant point higher than that of teammate Mike Brocki. Regina's player-coach Jason Felice, a triple-crown winner the previous year, placed third in the race for the batting title, hitting a robust .394 with twenty-three homers and eighty RBIs.

Regina topped Moose Jaw to advance to the finals against the well-rested and heavily favoured Aberdeen Pheasants. Suprisingly the Cyclones emerged as champions, capturing the best-of-five series three games to one. Regina's Jim Cafferty chose the ideal time to hit his first home run of the season, launching a game-winning round-tripper in the top of the twelfth inning in the deciding contest.

The Prairie League suffered through the normal growing pains of a first-year circuit. Moose Jaw was the top draw, attracting seventy-five thousand fans, followed by Regina with fifty thousand. Brandon could not recover from its slow start and drew fewer than twenty-five thousand supporters. Still the league is optimistic about next season. Red Deer has been approached to join the league and Moose Jaw Diamond Dog general manager Arnold Asham, a native Manitoban, is even considering putting a team in Stonewall, Manitoba.

In 1994, years of frustration ended for Sam Katz when he and his partners Jeff Thompson and the Winnipeg Enterprises Corporation purchased the Rochester Aces and moved the team to Winnipeg. For ten years Katz had tried in vain to land a Triple A franchise for Winnipeg, only to be told that city lacked the proximity to other ball clubs. Now at long last he had landed a franchise in the independent Double A calibre Northern League.

The league had a definite blue-collar appeal with a salary cap set at $72,000. Tickets were inexpensive and fans could relate to players motivated by a shot at being signed into a major league or playing for the sheer love of the game. The league introduced a twenty-second clock between pitches to speed up play. Team rosters had to meet certain stipulations: each club could carry four veterans with more than four years' experience in a major-league system; two players were entitled to have four years' professional service; and six players had to be rookies. In 1993, the league's first year of operation, the gamble of accepting very short money for the chance of some exposure had panned out for thirty-seven players.

Winnipeg returned to the name Goldeyes for its newest incarnation, with its opposition in the Northern League coming from St. Paul, Duluth, Sioux City, Sioux Falls, and Thunder Bay. The American clubs featured some faded major-leaguers like Pedro Guerrero, Leon Durham, and Dennis "Oil Can" Boyd. Winnipeg coach Doug Siminuc, the former skipper of the Rochester Aces, wisely chose to avoid a marquee player, signing experienced journeymen like catcher Dan Bilardello and pitchers Rich Thompson and Jeff Bittiger. Siminuc made certain that Tim Cain came over to the club as one of the protected picks from the dispersion of Rochester's players.

To say that Winnipeg was enthusiastic about the return of pro ball would be an understatement. Fewer people have turned out for Bomber football games than the 14,758 supporters who turned out for the Goldeyes' home opener against the Duluth Dukes. Tim Cain repaid the club's confidence in him by pitching a masterful outing. The game was deadlocked at one apiece in the bottom of the fifth inning when the Goldeyes erupted for seven runs, enabling Cain to cruise to a 9-1 triumph.

I'd been out of town for that first game, checking out the ballparks in Calgary and Edmonton as part of my research. My memories of going to games as a kid remain some of the most precious of my life, so I was ill-prepared for the totally charmless, carpet-covered, badly proportioned kennel that greeted me upon entering Winnipeg's alleged field. Happily the sentimental meanderings of one middle-aged fan did not impact upon the team, and fan support far outstripped the owners' expectations. The Goldeyes averaged six thousand fans in the first half of the season despite not faring particularly well in the win column.

Tim Cain was the club's lone bright spot; however, his 5-1 record with a sparkling 2.30 ERA drew the attention of the Boston Red Sox, who bought Cain's contract and shipped him to their Double A New Britain affiliate. This was a blow to the team, but a clear indicator to the players that there were opportunities out there.

The Goldeyes did not stand pat waiting for the team to improve, but shipped first-sacker Warren Sackiw, the lone Canadian player on their roster, to the Thunder Bay Whisky Jacks for Tim Bruce, a fine rookie pitcher. They continued to juggle the line-up, bringing in veteran slugger Jim Wilson to shore up the designated-hitter spot, then managing to pry 1993 Rookie of the Year Steve Dailey away from Duluth. Siminuc found the right mix as the club rebounded, capturing the second half of the season.

The steady revolving of the turnstiles was not limited only to Winnipeg. Organized baseball was forced to sit up and take notice when the independent Northern League shattered the short-season attendance record of 797,993 set by the Northwest League the previous season. The St. Paul's Saints broke the Salt Lake City Trappers' attendance record of 217,268, while Winnipeg drew over 212,000.

The Goldeyes opened the playoffs in Sioux City, rallying from a 3-0 deficit to capture the crucial first game of the series. Winnipeg trounced the Explorers in the second contest, returning to Winnipeg with the opportunity to become the first local professional sports team since the 1978 W.H.A. Jets to clinch a title at home. A throng of eighty-four hundred fans turned out in anticipation of a Goldeye series sweep but the Explorers kept the corks in the champagne bottles with a 6-3 triumph.

I ended my boycott of the field from hell, attending the fourth game of the series with over seventy-three hundred ball fans. Tim Bruce drew

"Bilardello's Championship Swing"
Catcher Dan Bilardello unloads on a grand slam that clinches the Northern League championship for the Winnipeg Goldeyes.

the starting assignment for Winnipeg and pitched brilliantly. The score was tied at one apiece in the bottom of the fourth when Pete Coachman, another mid-season acquisition, cranked a solo homer to left. The inning was far from over, however; Sioux City opted to walk Mike Hankins intentionally to load the bases, with Dan Bilardello, a sixteen-year veteran of the baseball wars, standing in the on-deck circle. Sioux City paid for this slight. Bilardello worked Benny Puig to a two-and-two count before depositing a fastball into the bleachers. That for all intents and purposes was the game as Winnipeg strolled to an 8-1 victory. Jim Wilson was declared the series MVP in his final game as a professional.

I can't claim to have become caught up in the moment, finding myself transported back into my youth, nor did a ballpark I detest suddenly turn into Wrigley Field. To me the lasting memory of the evening will be Goldeye reliever Todd Marion dropping to his knees, looking skyward, after recording the final out. It will be the unbridled joy of the players as they swarmed the mound, hollering and hugging

"Yes"
Todd Marion drops to his knees
in joy after striking out the final
Sioux City batter to clinch an 8-1
championship game triumph on
September 9, 1994.

each other. Let's face it, their happiness wasn't about money or going to Disney World; the kid selling popcorn in the stands was probably pulling in a bigger buck than the players. That night was about baseball – the game, not business.

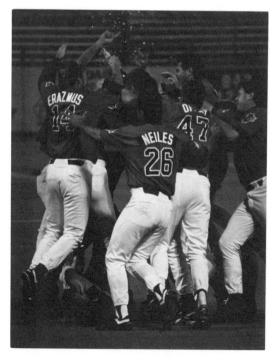

"Pandemonium Reigns"
Goldeyes explode from the
dugout to celebrate on the
mound.

Winnipeg had nothing to fear from the sophomore jinx in 1995. The Goldeyes drew 195,000 fans but generated even more revenue than the previous season. The club established a Northern League record by swatting 102 home runs during the season, paced by its slugging first baseman Terry Lee. Lee had twice been up with the Cincinnati Reds for the proverbial cup of coffee and even owned a 1990 World Series ring. He had spent the previous year out of baseball, working in a hardware store in his home town of Eugene, Oregon. The strike brought him out of retirement for a final fling as a replacement player and eventually to Winnipeg, where he captured two-thirds of the triple crown with a league-leading .376 batting average and seventy-three RBIs. He was runner-up to Duluth's Pete Kuld with twenty-two homers, making him the deserving winner of the league MVP honours.

The St. Paul's Saints repeated as the circuit's top draw, winning both halves of the regular season. This meant that the team with the second-best overall record would advance to the final. Winnipeg and Sioux City finished with identical records, setting up a sudden-death clash. Goldeye catcher Hank Manning cranked out a round-tripper in the top of the tenth that sent Winnipeg to the final for the second year in a row. It would mark the third straight trip to the finals for Goldeye manager Doug Siminuc, a gruff, tobacco-chewing *hombre* who seemed to have a knack of alienating local fans. It was a rocky year for some of the players and Goldeye fans. Shortstop Ken Arnold got a little fed up with being booed and gave the crowd the finger one night. Centre-fielder Daryl Brinkley referred to a patron as a "fat fuck" during another contest. Siminuc and pitching coach Jeff Bittiger were ordered to make a formal apology to the fans for criticizing their knowledge of the game in the press. Personally I've never felt that buying a ticket to an event gave people the right to heap abuse on the performers. I recall John Robertson's superb column in the *Winnipeg Tribune* in the 1960s stating that most of us are afforded the luxury of a few errors at work without being held up to ridicule.

The media-orchestrated rift between the players and fans clearly had little negative effect at the turnstiles. The Goldeyes established a short-season single-game attendance mark, drawing 20,739 spectators out to their final regular-season home game. The crowd was larger than those at six of the major-league games played that evening.

Twin Cities baseball fans had their choice of clubs to root for when the final series opened in St. Paul. The Twins were playing over at the hapless "Baggy Dome" that day, managing a whopping twenty-seven hundred fans. The well-marketed and winning Saints outdrew their major-league counterparts by two thousand fans, taking the series opener 3-2. Winnipeg flew starter Darren McLellan in from his University of Florida college campus in Gainesville to pitch the second contest. He rebounded from a shaky start, giving up three runs in the first inning, to pitch 6⅔ innings, giving up four runs en route to a 6-4 victory. The Los Angeles Lakers may have Jack Nicholson following them on road trips but Winnipeg fans were treated to the sight of Bill Murray, a part owner in the St. Paul club, sitting in the bleachers cheering on his team. In the third game, Winnipeg centre-fielder Daryl Brinkley made like Long John Silver, scaling the netting in deep left-centre to rob Greg D'Alexander of a grand-slam homer, but a pair of solo shots by Doug O'Neill provided the margin of victory in a 2-0 Saints win. St. Paul's pitching proved too strong for the Goldeyes as the Saints captured their second Northern League championship in three years with a 4-0 triumph in the fourth and deciding game.

The Saints, with their unprecedented popularity, were profiled on the critically acclaimed television show *60 Minutes*. It was refreshing to hear club owner Mike Veeck say that by the time a ballplayer knocks on his door, he has one foot out of baseball. It is this kind of realistic attitude that will enable the club to remain successful. The Northern League has six healthy franchises going into its fourth year of operation. Every club, with the exception of Duluth-Superior, drew over 100,000 fans. St. Paul obliterated its own short-season attendance mark by drawing over a quarter of a million supporters. The ranks will swell to include clubs in Fargo, North Dakota, and Madison, Wisconsin, in 1996. Fargo has already signed Doug Siminuc to guide its club through its inaugural season. A few weeks later Winnipeg got Fargo's first-round draft pick for the rights to Jeff Bittiger.

It is interesting to note that the crowd of four thousand fans that turned out to witness the Goldeyes' final loss in the series to St. Paul was no larger than the crowd that took in the first Maroons game against Cavalier in 1902. This is the message that minor-league owners on the Prairies must heed: set realistic attendance expectations of four or five thousand fans. Despite the constant refrain by our mayor that Winnipeg is a world-class city, we are in fact a minor-league town. This point was graphically driven home during the fiasco over the departure of the Winnipeg Jets.

When I began the research for this book in the spring of 1994, major-league baseball was experiencing unprecedented success at the box office. Now, a year and a half later, fans are still bitter over the greed that managed to cancel a World Series, a feat that two World Wars could not accomplish. Attendance is down by thirty percent and the "show" no longer has the sponsorship of a national American television network. Team ownership is ceasing to be the plaything of the very wealthy and has become an investment for multinational corporations.

Nearing the end of the 1995 season, Kevin Malone, vice-president and general manager of the Montreal Expos, told an interviewer in *Christian Week* that professional baseball is being controlled by Satan. While not a reason that I had considered for the game's sudden decline, the major leagues in their present state are doomed. There are half a dozen teams, Montreal included, that can't support a franchise.

During the same time frame, owning a minor-league ball club on the Canadian Prairies has become something of a cottage industry. The owners of these teams are owed a debt of gratitude; theirs is not an enterprise to guarantee entry into the Fortune 500. Unfortunately the vagaries of minor-league sport are cyclical by nature. Even a winning team, sophisticatedly marketed, cannot prevent fan apathy. There are currently more pro teams on the Prairies than ever before. Do yourself a favour and take in a game!

The fundamentals have not changed much since the professional game debuted on the Prairies in 1886. The pitcher's mound is still sixty feet six inches from home plate and the bases are ninety feet apart. Bats are still made of turned ash and the ball is still covered in horsehide or cowhide. Fortunately the practice of infielders cutting base runners out at the knees has long since disappeared, and no umpire has had the diamond surrounded by irate fans in recent memory. Betting and booze have nipped at the underbelly of pro sports since their inception.

Kids still collect baseball cards but now with an eye to their fiduciary capacity. Gone are the days of poring longingly through a shoebox filled with your favourite players. Now cards must be maintained in mint condition while being stored in binders under plastic sleeves. There are no favourite players, only cards that will appreciate in value.

When I was growing up the thrill of going to the ballpark was the game itself. Now a sport that should be able to stand on its own merit has to be slickly packaged as family entertainment. In our media-driven society the average concentration span is a thirty-second sound byte. The last couple of games that I went to, the kids seemed to spend more time following the mascot around than watching the action on the field.

As luck would have it, my bus ride home from work each day passes the field that I played on as a child. No matter how foul the weather or black my mood, a mere glimpse of that ball field transports me back to the carefree days of my boyhood. The memories are no longer those of a lamenting ex-jock trading on past glories, but rather of fresh air, laughter, and my buddies. I still get out and shag flies every so often and it remains to me one of the simple pleasures of life.

Canadian Prairie Teams

ALBERTA

Bassano
1912	Boosters, Western Canada League

Calgary
1907	Broncos, Western Canada League
1909	Cowpunchers or Eyeopeners, Western Canada League
1910–14	Broncos, Western Canada League
1920–21	Broncos, Western Canada League
1922	Broncos, Western International League
1947–50	Purity 99s and Buffaloes, Big Four Inter-City League
1953–54	Stampeders, Western International League
1960	Buffaloes, Western Canada League
1963-64	Giants, Western Canada League
1977–78	Cardinals, Pioneer League
1979–84	Expos, Pioneer League
1985–	Cannons, Pacific Coast League

Edmonton
1907	Grays, Western Canada League
1909–11	Eskimos, Western Canada League
1912–13	Gray Birds or Grays, Western Canada League
1914	Eskimos, Western Canada League
1920	Esquimos, Western Canada League
1921	Eskimos, Western Canada League
1922	Eskimos, Western International League
1947–50	Eskimos, Big Four Inter-City League
1947-49	Cubs, Big Four Inter-City League
1950	Dodgers, Big Four Inter-City League
1953–54	Eskimos, Western International League
1955–58	Eskimos, Western Canada League
1959	Eskimos, Can. Am. League
1961	Oilers, Western Canada League
1963–64	Oilers, Western Canada League
1981–	Trappers, Pacific Coast League

Lethbridge
1907	Lethbridge, Western Canada League
1909–11	Miners, Western Canada League

1960–61	White Sox, Western Canada League
1963–64	Cardinals, Western Canada League
1975–76	Expos, Pioneer League
1977–83	Dodgers, Pioneer League
1992–	Mounties, Pioneer League

Medicine Hat

1907	Hatters, Western Canada League
1909–10	Mad Hatters, Western Canada League
1913–14	Hatters, Western Canada League
1951	Mohawks, Western Canada League
1961	Meridians, Western Canada League
1963	Commodores, Western Canada League
1977	A's, Pioneer League
1978–	Blue Jays, Pioneer League

Red Deer

| 1912 | Eskimos, Western Canada League |

MANITOBA

Brandon

1903	Brandon, Manitoba Senior Baseball League
1908	Angels, Northern League
1909–11	Angels, Western Canada League
1933–34	Greys, Northern League
1948–54	Greys, Man Dak League
1995–	Grey Owls, Prairie League

Carman

| 1950–54 | Carman Cardinals, Man Dak League |

St. Boniface

| 1915 | St. Boniface Saints, Northern League |

Winnipeg

1886	C.P.R., Metropolitan and Hotel clubs, Manitoba Baseball League
1891	C.P.R., Metropolitan and Hotel clubs, Red River Valley League
1902–05	Maroons or Pegs or Brownies, Northern League
1906–07	Maroons or Pegs or Brownies, North Copper Country League
1908	Maroons or Pegs or Brownies, Northern League
1909–11	Maroons or Pegs or Brownies, Western Canada League
1912	Maroons or Pegs or Brownies, Central International League

1913–17	Maroons or Pegs or Brownies, Northern League
1919–21	Maroons, Western Canada League
1933–42	Maroons, Northern League
1947–50	Elmwood Giants, Manitoba League
1950–51	Elmwood Giants and Buffaloes, Man Dak League
1952	Giants, Man Dak League
1953	Royals, Man Dak League
1954–64	Goldeyes, Northern League
1969	Goldeyes, Northern League
1970–71	Whips, International League
1994–	Goldeyes, Northern League

SASKATCHEWAN

Estevan

1951	Maple Leafs, Western Canada League
1952	Maple Leafs, Saskatchewan League

Indian Head

1953–54	Rockets, Saskatchewan League

Lloydminster

1953–54	Meridians, Saskatchewan League
1955–57	Meridians, Western Canada League
1958	Combines (with North Battleford), Western Canada League
1959	Combines (with North Battleford), Can. Am. League
1960	Meridians, Western Canada League

Moose Jaw

1909–11	Robin Hoods, Western Canada League
1913–14	Robin Hoods, Western Canada League
1919–20	Robin Hoods, Western Canada League
1921	Millers, Western Canada League
1951	Canucks, Western Canada League
1952	Maple, Saskatchewan League
1955–58	Mallards, Western Canada League
1995–	Diamond Dogs, Prairie League

North Battleford

1952–54	Beavers, Saskatchewan League
1955–57	Beavers, Western Canada League
1958	Combines (with Lloyminster), Western Canada League
1959	Combines (with Lloydminster), Can. Am. League

Regina

1909–11	Bonepilers, Western Canada League
1913–14	Red Sox, Western Canada League
1919–21	Senators, Western Canada League
1951	Caps, Western Canada League
1952–54	Caps, Saskatchewan League
1955–58	Braves, Western Canada League
1959	Senators, Can. Am. League
1994	Cyclones, independent North Central League
1995–	Cyclones, Prairie League

Rosetown

1954	Phillies, Saskatchewan League

Saskatoon

1910	Berry Pickers, Western Canada League
1911	Quakers, Western Canada League
1913	Quakers, Western Canada League
1914	Sheiks, Western Canada League
1919–21	Quakers, Western Canada League
1952–54	Gems, Saskatchewan League
1955–58	Gems, Western Canada League
1959	Commodores, Can. Am. League
1960–61	Commodores, Western Canada League
1964	Blues, Western Canada League
1994	Riot, independent North Central League
1995–	Riot, Prairie League

Leagues on the Canadian Prairies

Northern Copper Country League
Winnipeg, MB   1906–1907, 1994–

Northern League
Brandon, MB   1908, 1933–34
St. Boniface, MB   1915
Winnipeg, MB   1903–05, 1908, 1913–17, 1933–42, 1954–64, 1969

Western Canada League
Bassano, AB   1912
Brandon, MB   1909–11
Calgary, AB   1907, 1909–14, 1920–21
Edmonton, AB   1907, 1909–14, 1920–21
Lethbridge, AB   1907, 1909–11
Medicine Hat, AB   1907, 1909–10, 1913–14
Moose Jaw, SK   1909–11, 1913–14, 1919–21
Red Deer, AB   1912
Regina, SK   1909–11, 1913–14, 1919–21
Saskatoon, SK   1910–11, 1913–14, 1919–21
Winnipeg, MB   1909–11, 1919–21

Western International League
Calgary, AB   1922, 1953–54
Edmonton, AB   1922, 1953–54

Big Four Inter-City League
Calgary, AB   1947–50
Edmonton, AB   1947–50

Western Canada Baseball League (also called Western Canada League)
Calgary, AB   1960, 1963–64
Edmonton, AB   1955–58, 1961, 1963–64
Estevan, SK   1951
Lethbridge, AB   1960–61, 1963–64
Lloydminster, SK   1955–58, 1960
Medicine Hat, AB   1951, 1961, 1963
Moose Jaw, SK   1951, 1955–58
North Battleford, SK   1955–58
Regina, SK   1951, 1955–58
Saskatoon, SK   1955–58, 1960–61, 1964

Saskatchewan League

Estevan, SK	1952
Indian Head, SK	1953–54
Moose Jaw, SK	1952
Lloydminster, SK	1953–54
North Battleford, SK	1952–54
Regina, SK	1952–54
Rosetown, SK	1954
Saskatoon, SK	1952–54

Can. Am. League

Edmonton, SK	1959
Lloydminster/	
North Battleford, SK	1959
Regina, SK	1959
Saskatoon, SK	1959

Sources

Chadwick, Bruce. *When the Game Was Black and White*. New York: Abbeville Press, 1992.

Clark, Dick, and Larry Lester. *The Negro Leagues Book*. Cleveland: Society for American Baseball Research, 1994.

Coleman, MacDonald. *The Face of Yesterday: The Story of Brandon, Manitoba*. Brandon, Man.: Leech Printing, 1957.

Duncan, Hal G. *Baseball in Manitoba*. Souris, Man.: Sanderson Printing, 1989.

Green, Wilson F. *Red River Revelations*. Fargo, N.D.: Red River Valley Historical Society, 1974.

Healy, William J. *Women of Red River*. Winnipeg: Russell, Lang and Co. Ltd., 1923.

Honig, Donald. *Shadows of Summer: Classic Baseball Photographs, 1869–1947*. New York: Viking Studio Books, 1994.

Humber, William. *Cheering for the Home Team*. Erin, Ont.: Boston Mills Press, 1983.

Humber, William. *Diamonds of the North*. New York: Oxford University Press, 1995.

Johnson, Lloyd. *Baseball's Dream Teams: The Greatest Players Decade by Decade*. New York: Gallery Books, 1990.

Johnson, Lloyd, and Brenda Ward. *Who's Who in Baseball History*. Greenwich: Brompton Books Corp., 1994.

Johnson, Lloyd, and Miles Wolff. *The Encyclopedia of Minor League Baseball*. Durham: Baseball America, Inc., 1993.

MacPhail, Colin. *Edmonton Trappers Media Guide*. Edmonton: Edmonton Trappers, 1994.

Nett, David S. and Richard M. Cohen, eds. *The Sports Encyclopedia: Baseball*. 11th ed. New York: St. Martin's Press, 1991.

Paige, Leroy (Satchel). *Maybe I'll Pitch Forever*. Lincoln: University of Nebraska Press, 1993.

Spalding, Albert G. *America's National Game*. Lincoln: University of Nebraska Press, 1992.

Traub, John H. *Calgary Cannons Media Guide*. Calgary: Calgary Cannons, 1994.

Vincent, Ted. *The Rise and Fall of American Sports*. Lincoln: University of Nebraska Press, 1994.

Ward, Geoffrey C., and Ken Burns. *Baseball: An Illustrated History*. New York: Alfred A. Knopf, 1994.

Palmer, Pete and John Thorn, eds. *Total Baseball: The Ultimate Encyclopedia of Baseball*. 3rd ed. New York: Harper Perennial, 1993.

Index

Photograph and Illustration Credits

The cooperation of persons and organizations in providing photographs and illustrations, and permission to reproduce them, is gratefully appreciated. The pages on which photographs or illustrations appear are listed after each source.

Calgary Cannons Baseball Club, 61, 88 and 94.

Department of Archives and Special Collections, University of Manitoba, 20 and 24 (PC 58 No. 0075).

Edmonton Trappers Baseball Club, 60 (*Action Photography*), 90 and 104 (*Denyse Conroy*).

Glenbow Archives, Calgary, Alberta, 35 (*NA 1276-1*), 38 (*NA 5329-17*), 43 (*NC 6-4725*) and 44 (*NA 3965-13*).

Metz Family Collection, 62 and 65.

Provincial Archives of Alberta, 29 (*A3115*), 32 (*A11,952*), 36 (*A7257*), 39 (*A11,952*), 52 (*A7284*), 70 (*A7270*) and 85 (*7266*).

Provincial Archives of Manitoba, 34 top (*Manitoba Sports Hall of Fame 169*), 34 bottom (*Winnipeg Parks N5328*), 42 (*Floods N12526*), 47 (*Foote N2654-1*), 50 (*Manitoba Sports Hall of Fame 170*), 76 (*Manitoba Sports Hall of Fame 172*) and 81 (*Manitoba Sports Hall of Fame 172*).

Saskatchewan Archives Board, 2 (*R-A3654*), 10 (*R-B10206*), 26 (*R-B1859*), 27 (*R-A3654*), 28 (*R-B10206*), 30 (*R-A6551-2*), 41 (*R-A17240*), 51 (*R-A7115*) and 53 (*R-B2886-2*).

Jeff Solylo, 74 top and bottom, 102, 111, and 112 top and bottom.

University of Nebraska Press, from *America's National Game* by Albert G. Spalding, 4, 9, 12, 14 and 19.

Western Canada Pictorial Index, 46 (*Winnipeg Free Press 2186-38501*), 55 (*Winnipeg Free Press 1238-37063*), 56 (*Winnipeg Free Press 1240-37123*), 58 (*Winnipeg Free Press 1193-35713*)and 68 (*C.N.R. 1811-42757*).

Life in the nineties is all too often a high inside fast ball that leaves you reeling in the dirt. I've always fancied myself as a fifties kind of guy, more intrigued by radio than the Internet. I wouldn't trade my childhood for anything and playing ball is a big part of those memories. I lived through many a cold winter by just sniffing my ball glove to conjure up images of springtime.

Time, age and the further deterioration of my always limited abilities prevent me from playing organized baseball any more. However, I still pore over the box scores and devour all the highlight packages, and feel ever so younger and happier with each "Opening Day."

Lewis St. George Stubbs is a freelance researcher and archival assistant at the University of Manitoba. He is the author of *Hockey Twenty Years* (Doubleday) and *A Majority of One* (Queenston House).